Feb 2019

D0742995

COMPANIONS
IN CONFLICT

COMPANIONS IN CONFLICT

Animals in Occupied Palestine

PENNY JOHNSON

MELVILLE HOUSE
BROOKLYN · LONDON

COMPANIONS IN CONFLICT

Copyright © 2019 by Penny Johnson

Map is courtesy of Good Shepherd Engineering and Palestine
Mapping Center Beit Jala Palestine.
(www.gsecc.com / www.palmap.org / info@gse.ps)

First Melville House Printing: February 2019

Melville House Publishing
46 John Street
Brooklyn, NY 11201
and
Suite 2000
16/18 Woodford Rd.
London E7 0HA

mhpbooks.com
@melvillehouse

ISBN: 978-1-61219-743-2
ISBN: 978-1-61219-744-9 (ebook)

Designed by Betty Lew

Printed in the United States of America

2 4 6 8 10 9 7 5 3 1

A catalog record for this book is available
from the Library of Congress

To Bruce Johnson (1950–2006),
who was kinder to animals than to himself

CONTENTS

Donkey grazing in an olive grove near Ramallah, April 2017.
(Credit: Emile Ashrawi)

COMMON LIVES

"I wish I was a donkey," said the great Palestinian poet Mahmoud Darwish in a television interview in 1997, pointing to a scrawny donkey standing under an olive tree near the Palestinian town of Ramallah. "A peaceful, wise animal that pretends to be stupid. Yet he is patient, and smarter than we are in the cool and calm manner he watches on as history unfolds." But in the history-laden and often heartbroken land between the Mediterranean Sea and the Jordan River—now the state of Israel and occupied Palestine—does the donkey watch so placidly as humans go their troubled way?

I do not think so. In this book, I explore the histories and intertwined fates of some of the large mammals that live in this fractured land—hyenas, goats, camels, sheep, gazelles, wild boars, ibexes, jackals, and donkeys, along with a pack of wolves, a solitary leopard, and several herds of cows, real and imagined. I encounter both wild and working animals along the way, as well as those animals—sheep, goats, cows—which we generically and tellingly call livestock. Almost all, with the exception of a European breed of cow, have inhabited this land under all its human names for millennia, contributing to our very survival. The current threats to their lives and well-being differ, but all are our companions in conflict.

What do their lives and our long engagement with these animals, whether in fear and aggression, through dominion and domestication, or with empathy and affection, tell us about the unfolding of the history of Palestinians and Israelis and the future of our common land? What do the stories, poems, and folktales we weave around these animals tell us about ourselves?

As one of the inhabitants of this land, I am part of the story I am telling. I came to Ramallah in 1982 to work for a year at Birzeit University on human rights issues, and I have remained for more than three decades and perhaps for a lifetime. Palestine has offered me a challenging working life, whether sitting in military courtrooms with inspiring Israeli and Palestinian lawyers defending university students and staff, participating with colleagues and friends on campus in founding an Institute of Women's Studies, or traveling to Madrid in 1991 as a writer for the Palestine delegation to the Madrid Peace Conference, a moment of hope.

But two particular measures of these crucial decades have led me to think about the lives of animals other than humans in this fragile land: times of walking and times of war.

I often walk and wander (when wars will allow it), usually with my partner, Raja Shehadeh, both before and after our marriage in 1988 (walking, by the way, is conducive to courting). Our town of Ramallah rests on the hills of the central highlands—the spine that runs through the West Bank, a rather recent name for land west of the Jordan River. The terraced hills host olive groves and fruit trees, as well as wilder terrain visible as one descends through one of the numerous wadis (valleys), heading for a spring or simply a flat rock to sit on in the warm sunshine.

Some of the animals in this book are acquaintances from

these walks: gazelles seen with a leap of the heart, wild boars spotted with more than a tremor of fear, sheep grazing on winter green, and goats munching on our ubiquitous thorns in the heat of summer. In spring, donkeys plow under the olive trees and in autumn carry away the harvest. Mahmoud Darwish's donkey is even nearer, a neighbor down the street. Other walks have taken me farther: to the long wadis that cut through the Jerusalem wilderness and to the dramatic canyons above the Dead Sea. I have been fortunate as well to take walks in the Galilee, but for almost two decades I have not been able to enter Gaza, as I do not belong to one of the proper bureaucratic categories able to secure a permit to enter the other part of occupied Palestine: diplomats, staff of international organizations, foreign journalists, and occasional businessmen.

Over the years, I have experienced the changes visited upon the animal habitats in the occupied West Bank and beyond. Whether fleet gazelles or plodding donkeys, these animals went their own way amid the media fanfare that accompanied both the 1993 signing of the Declaration of Principles between Israel and The Palestine Liberation Organization on the White House lawn and the Interim Agreement two years later. They could not hide, though, from the ensuing dramatic changes—not only political but also physical—in the landscape that is their home. Those agreements, often termed the Oslo Accords or simply "Oslo," mandated a transitional period where certain civil responsibilities over the Palestinian population in the occupied West Bank and Gaza were transferred to a newly created Palestinian Authority, pending final status negotiations. A quarter of a century later, negotiations are frozen and the transitional arrangements have become what many call "occupation by another name." (And indeed, the Israeli military government was never dissolved.)

The West Bank was and still is fragmented into zones governed by an impersonal alphabet. Area A, where the Palestinian Authority has full control (more in theory than in practice), constitutes only 18 percent of the West Bank (excluding Jerusalem) and is a patchwork of unconnected urban centers and a scattering of villages. Area B, where Palestinian security personnel can only operate with Israeli permission, contains the majority of Palestinian villages, frequently not including all of any given village's agricultural and grazing land. The most unfortunate Palestinian communities, as well as most of the land's wildlife, lie in Area C, the 61 percent of the West Bank under sole Israeli control and the location of more than one hundred Israeli settlements. Here, I explore what this complex period has meant not only for those of us who walk and cherish the land but for the lives of wild and working animals and the humans who depend on them.

My second measure of time is war and conflict: Raja and I once counted the wars since our wedding, celebrated at the height of the First Palestinian Intifada, a mass civil anti-occupation uprising that began in December 1987. At first we decided wars came neatly in twos: two intifadas (the second of which erupted in 2000, wracked with violence and despair), two Gulf Wars (in 1990 and 2003), two Gaza Wars, and two major wars between Israel and Lebanon (the first back in 1982, the last in 2006). But then we looked around us at regional conflagrations and promptly lost count. The losses of human lives and livelihoods can be tallied by statisticians and mourned by citizens, but it is time, I think, to reflect as well on the massive destruction visited on our animal companions and the environment that sustains us all.

Writing in a year marking the fiftieth anniversary of Israel's military occupation of the West Bank and Gaza, I am all too aware of what we humans, Palestinians and those of us who live in Palestine, have in common with other mammals: a disturbing, even frightening, loss of habitat. I explore how the lives of animals help us understand what is happening to all of us. Sipping cardamom-scented coffee, I hear from shepherds in the southern Hebron Hills how a new geography of exclusion threatens not only their livelihoods but the existence of their community. Reflecting on the human fear and loathing of hyenas and the near-reflexive reaction to kill these vulnerable creatures, I visit a military court and prison complex near Ramallah and think about connections as I observe young Palestinian men on trial.

Animal lives can illuminate human hopes, fears, and absurdities in a small land scarred by conflict and occupation: whether a herd of cows chased by the Israeli military as a security threat, a camel arrested in Jerusalem for not having a permit, or, alas, a donkey loaded with explosives. And human activities deeply affect the prospects of mammalian survival, whether the building of a Wall the march of Israeli hilltop settlements, or the urban sprawl in Palestinian towns. Our decisions—going to war or going to work, herding goats as a millenia-old practice or starting a modern dairy farm as a new economic enterprise, developing nature reserves or planning land use for political ends—transform the lives of our animal companions.

But animals are more than passive reactors to human action. Equally important are the *shared* lives of humans and animals on the ground today and over many centuries. At a time when large mammals are vanishing around the globe— and are extremely threatened in a Middle East region wracked by war, desertification, and devastation—the story of humans, animals, and crisis in Palestine/Israel has a particular urgency in both the present and the past tense.

Indeed, the past can tell us not only what is lost but what can be recovered in a land which, although so small, encompasses a wide variety of environments. Palestine/Israel ranges from desert to central highlands to fertile plains to the Great Rift Valley, from a life-sustaining lake to the stark beauty of the shrinking Dead Sea—all habitats for the mammals under discussion. And humans live and work in equally diverse (and contradictory) environments, including the highly developed economy of Israel, the "developing" and severely constrained economy of Palestine under occupation (or more accurately the West Bank), and the "de-developed" and besieged world of Gaza, each with varying strains on both human and animal life.

Exploring the long and rich encounter of Palestinians and working animals opens up all these diverse physical and economic environments. In much of Europe and the United States, working animals have all but disappeared; in Palestine, they have only quite recently vanished from some urban landscapes (and in fuel-strapped Gaza City, donkey and mule carts are frequently resurrected as alternative taxis). The camels who once hauled oranges to the Jaffa port (and who in 1913 played a part in one of the first clashes between new Jewish settlers and Palestinian villagers) are now largely banished to the desert along with their Bedouin companions, those nomadic (now semi-nomadic) Arabs that were and are integral to Palestine and the region. Camels now appear as working animals for tourists, perched in melancholy splendor along the road to the Dead Sea and on the Mount of Olives. Once-ubiquitous donkeys, the most hardworking of human companions, now toil for the Palestinian poor in villages and Bedouin encampments where water is still hauled and life is on the margin. And there is no getting around goats, which still number about a quarter of a million in the West Bank alone. They were once declared "Public Enemy No. 1" by the British Mandate authorities who ruled the region between the two World Wars and who viewed the admittedly voracious goat as a main obstacle to transforming "desolate" Palestine into a green and pleasant land. The long tradition of animal folklore has also etched working and wild animals and the characters given to them into the imagination of rural and urban dwellers alike.

The human–animal relationship is deeply embedded in both our histories and our psyches and is lost at our peril. The common lives—and common graves—of humans and animals, stretching back to the early Stone Age and explored in this book, attest to that. Henning Mankell, in his moving memoir *Quicksand*, written as he faced his own mortality after a diagnosis of lung cancer, wrote of his visit to the underground caves and tunnels in Sweden where toxic nuclear waste is stored. Warning of the destructive potential of these caves, he invoked the rock carvings of animals upon these and similar cave walls as the birthplace of art:

There is a common denominator in nearly all the cave paintings that exist, and it is also characteristic of our own rock carvings in Sweden: the animals depicted are created in great detail. Their eyes shine, their movements are reproduced dynamically. But when human beings are depicted they are mostly no more than unfinished sketches. Matchbook figures hastily produced, as if more detailed pictures were not necessary. One can speculate about the reason for that, of course, but in all probability it is simply because the animals were more important.

I write as scientists, philosophers, and we ordinary humans are more engaged than ever in studying and reflecting on animal behavior. Certainly the notion of an unbreachable boundary between humans and other animals has been decisively challenged. Many of the traits once thought uniquely human are now acknowledged to be shared with other animals, as various animals pass the tests humans administer, from tool use to mirror self-recognition. These animals to date have not examined us: I doubt that any human could pass a cat test and land on his or her feet after falling off a roof. I thus enjoy primatologist Frans de Waal turning the tables in the title of his recent book: *Are We Smart Enough to Know How Smart Animals Are?* De Waal also urges an evolutionary understanding of how each species develops physical, cognitive, and emotional capabilities to advance survival in a particular ecology or world. All these advances in understanding of animal cognition, sentience, emotion, and social behavior underlie my approach to the lives of large mammals in Palestine/Israel and the stories they tell me. I do not treat the science in any detail, but I have certainly benefitted from it. The burgeoning literature on animal rights is also in the background of my exploration and comes to the fore in my final chapter on prospects for environmental, animal welfare, and animal conservation initiatives in Palestine. However, I am most at home in this book not with the rights arguments, important as they are, but with the philosopher Cora Diamond's focus on "our response to animals as our fellows in mortality, in life on this earth," in my case the "earth" of a very particular place.

The whisper of extinct or nearly extinct wild animals, whether the last leopard in a deep wadi near the Dead Sea or the roll call of animals that vanished when the new state of Israel enthusiastically drained the Huleh wetlands in the 1950s, runs through the book. I consider the lives and environments of three still wild but threatened animals: gazelles, wolves, and ibexes—the elegant wild goats that inhabit the canyons above the Dead Sea. Wild animals that are flourishing—some to the extent of being considered infestations, such as wild boars and jackals—open up an inquiry into those animals who adapt to our garbage-strewn, overheated world, the new "inheritors of the earth," as biologist Chris Thomas calls them. I consider how jackals figure in the imagination of one of the region's most enduring cycle of tales, in a Kafka parable, and in a troubled story by Israeli writer Amos Oz.

The whispers of less vocal wild animals may be hard to hear amid the clamor of human needs and demands in a century-old conflict and fifty years of military occupation. Exploring attitudes and anecdotes from Palestinians living under military occupation sharply raises the question of how animal welfare and protection can be advanced when humans are suffering. "We are human beings" is perhaps the most common refrain from Palestinians facing humiliating treatment at the hands of a bored soldier at a checkpoint. And "animals" is the most frequent curse an angry Palestinian will hurl against the harsh behavior of Israeli soldiers or settlers. Humans here are the opposite of animals. Darwish's wish to be a donkey reverses this logic and is particularly resonant since *donkey* is an epithet for those deemed slow, stupid, or just plain obdurate.

Can humans engaged in conflict—and Palestinians living under military occupation—be concerned with the lives and welfare of other mammals? I will look not only at new environmental and animal welfare initiatives among Palestinians, introducing both activists and skeptics, but also at deep-rooted attitudes toward animals among older Palestinian peasants who work (and sometimes live) with animals, young Palestinians in cities who have never seen a gazelle, and Palestinians in villages who fear the incursion of wild boars, convinced they have been let loose by Israeli settlers. But, in my conclusion, I address the last, most difficult question to myself and to others I have met along the way: What conditions do we need, for humans as well as other mammals, for our common lives to flourish?

COMPANIONS IN CONFLICT

Camel and Bedouin guide resting at Mar Saba, a desert
monastery between Bethlehem and the Dead Sea.
(Credit: Gerard Horton)

CHAPTER 1

TAKE MY CAMEL: THE VANISHING CAMELS OF JERUSALEM AND JAFFA

Kojak was the most famous camel in Jerusalem. Accompanied by members of the camel-raising Abu Hawa family, Kojak plodded in the cloven hoof-steps of his father and grandfather, going to work on Jerusalem's Mount of Olives every day for more than two decades. Known as the "kissing camel" for his smooches with Abu Ismail, the patriarch of the Abu Hawa clan, he delighted tourists and gave them a panoramic saddle-top view of the Old City of Jerusalem and the Dome of the Rock. He entertained celebrities, even if minor ones: "Julio Iglesias stood right there," Abu Ismail once told an Israeli television reporter.

The Abu Hawa family originally had little trouble receiving a business license (for camel rides) from the Jerusalem municipality—given under a previous, more liberal, Israeli mayor, Teddy Kollek—but in 2009 Kojak's troubles began. The municipality rejected the license without explanation; thus the government vet would not give Kojak his vaccinations, and he was banned from Jerusalem. The official reasons included the lack of a business permit and "third party insurance." For all his grace, Kojak could not navigate the

Israeli bureaucracy, whose representatives, the Israeli police and veterinarian services, hauled him away in March 2011 and imprisoned him in a shack near the abandoned village of Lifta. The village's Palestinian residents fled in 1947 and 1948; it is now an Israeli nature reserve with a scattering of old stone houses the only reminder of its past.

Kojak's miseries have eerie parallels to the human predicaments of Palestinians living in a divided city. When Israel conquered the West Bank in the 1967 war, it unilaterally annexed Arab East Jerusalem. Its sovereignty there is not recognized by the international community, including the United States, although US President Trump seems to be a glaring exception. Palestinian Jerusalemites were given Israeli residency permits that, like Kojak's, are frequently under scrutiny and subject to revocation. For almost two decades now, Palestinians in the rest of the occupied West Bank have needed permits to enter Jerusalem.

For the first quarter century of military occupation, the West Bank and Gaza were closed military zones. They remain so today: a general exit permit issued annually by the Israeli military since 1972 used to allow movement to Jerusalem and Israel, but that general permit was cancelled in 1991. In the last two decades, Israel's "permit regime," as Israeli human rights lawyer Yael Berda calls it, has ever more closely regulated all forms of Palestinian mobility. Most dire is the situation of Palestinians in Gaza: a Swedish pediatric nurse at the Lutheran-run Augusta Victoria hospital in East Jerusalem almost wept as she told me about children from Gaza who came to the hospital for cancer treatment—but without their mothers, who were denied permission to accompany their sick children.

Unearthing how Kojak became an illegal immigrant in a city where he was born and bred is a window to a larger story of camels in Palestine and their human partners. Kojak was banished from Jerusalem by a direct bureaucratic order; the vanishing of camels from many urban and rural landscapes, however, was a complicated, century-long process. Icons of the Middle East and crucial to the caravans that crisscrossed the region, camels have provided transport for at least two thousand years, as well as milk, meat, and camel leather for their human companions. Shapers of cities and central to both urban trade and rural agriculture for so long, they have been exiled to the margins of most human spaces over the last century. Their story makes an ideal starting point for this book.

Looking back at the last century in Palestine—or even further—camels have been our companions in conflict, whether recruited in wartime in World War I or displaced as their habitat, occupation, and economy were drastically transformed in the twentieth century, first during the British Mandate over Palestine (1923–1948, preceded by British military administration from December 1917) and then with the dissolution of Palestine in 1948 and the emergence of the state of Israel. Today, the Israeli occupation of the West Bank and Gaza since 1967 holds the dismal record as the longest occupation in modern times and has had its own effects on camels and their human companions.

Was Kojak destined to be the last camel in Jerusalem? And where do camels belong, anyway? Turning onto the road that snakes along the Dead Sea, my husband Raja and I stopped at our favorite gas station near Qumran, the steep desert cliff dotted with caves, where the Dead Sea Scrolls were discovered in the late 1940s by Bedouin shepherds followed by very excited archeologists. This gas station boasts not one but two camels, available for tourist photo opportunities. I watched with fascination as a young camel took one long drink after another from a large plastic container, his Bedouin owner keeping pace with a hose. Camels can drink about twenty-seven gallons in ten minutes, an amount that would kill most other animals. In our contemporary imagination, camels are denizens of the desert, admirably suited for the region's arid terrain, given their unique ability to store water in their bloodstream.

Camels' ability to endure heavy loads and travel long distances without water, as well their fondness for eating thorns, are desert-friendly habits, although, as many distressed travelers confirm, eating camel thorn gives these animals acute halitosis. Geoffrey Inchbald, a historian of Britain's Imperial Camel Corps, which operated in Palestine during World War I, noted that "it is only the inexperienced who fail to take evasive action in time." And a tip if you are feeding a camel: the equally drought-resistant acacia plant does not have the same smelly effect and provides camels with the salt and water they need.

The numerous odd features of the camel, including sideways kicking, love of music, and unpredictable fits of irascibility, provoke mixed reactions among humans. Some are romantic. Reja-e Busailah, a blind boy growing up during the British Mandate, inhabited a world of sound. He remembers encountering a strange resonance when he and his family were camping near the sea during the Nebi Rubin festival. The sound was "low, deep, mellow and soothing," and Reja-e stumbled out of the tent to discover its source: a camel's voice. "This is how camels pray in the morning," an adult told him. Reja-e later compared it to "the cello's soft, deep tones." Traveling from Ramle to the coastal city of Jaffa in the late nineteenth century, Mary Eliza Rogers and her entourage encountered "a little company of Bedouin Arabs" feasting by the roadside. She described the mounted riders on their "unwieldy looking animals" harmonizing their songs to the monotonous swinging pace of their animals and the tinkling camel bells. They sang: "Dear unto me as the sight of my eyes art thou, oh my camel."

But a later British traveler and naturalist, Victor Howells, visiting Palestine at the end of World War II, had a more derogatory view. Howells depended on camels for transport on a trek through the Sinai and Negev (Naqab) Deserts but nonetheless heartily disliked the gray camel then prevalent in Palestine. An interesting idiosyncrasy peculiar to this particular camel breed, he observed, was "sudden fits of temper or temporary madness." He went on to describe an abrupt wave of hatred and rage that seized a previously peaceful camel standing under a tree in a small Arab village. The camel, according to Howells, became a "cyclone of lashing legs and snapping jaws" in his attack on an innocent donkey.

Even camel fans—those of us drawn to their unusual physique and curious character—can be seized with sudden doubt. In faraway Australia, writer Robyn Davidson opined that camels are "witty and endlessly charming." But then she was charged by a previously peaceful bull camel, who attacked her "like a windmill with teeth." My own experience, indeed my one and only camel ride, was less violent although still startling. Spring in Aswan in Upper Egypt being exceptionally mild and beautiful, I mounted a young camel for a romantic ride. He promptly reared his head, sniffed, and began to race into the desert, clearly in hot pursuit of female companionship. The equally young camel herders—after several fits of laughter—ran after him and, to my eternal gratitude, caught him. I dismounted with a giant thump. *Never again*, I thought, and so it was. Check gender before riding: another piece of advice from our Imperial Camel Corps historian. While not-

ing that the camel is a "wonderful and unique creature," Inchbald is clear that bull camels in rutting season—which, he says
ruefully, comes very often—are not only useless but dangerous, citing an incident in which a bull knelt on his rider in an
attempt to kill him.

But camels once roamed well beyond the desert and carried much more than slightly uneasy tourists. Camels are often
viewed as the premier animals of the arid Middle East, the "ships
of the desert," in one stock description, although the equivalent
idiomatic phrase in Arabic is simply "caravans of the desert."
But in a region that has been a crossroads for human migration
and has witnessed the rise and fall of civilizations throughout
history, camels were also immigrants, albeit ten million years
ago. Our camels' ancestors in the Camelidae family emerged in
North America some forty million years ago and roamed the
plains there for millions of years. Among their ranks, as Ken
Thompson points out, was the largest camel that ever lived,
standing at a height of eleven and a half feet and aptly named
Titanotylopus. Camelids with itchy feet crossed the land bridge
of the Bering Strait into Asia. Other camelid relatives filtered
into South America (think llamas). From Asia, our one-humped
camel (*Camelus dromdarius*, termed the Arabic camel) traveled farther, to the Arabian peninsula, while the two-humped
Bactrian camel evolved in the high mountains and plains of
Afghanistan and China. Indeed, we are all immigrants.

When the dromedary camel wandered from the sands of
Arabia into the Fertile Crescent and Palestine is not particularly clear. In the late nineteenth century, the British authors
of *The Survey of Western Palestine (1882–1888)* noted that the
camel "is bred abundantly on the plains of Moab [now Jor-
dan] and in southern Judea," and was present and employed
by humans in Syria from the earliest records. A recent investi-

gation by two Israeli archeologists, Erez Ben-Yosef and Lidar Sapir-Hen, caused a stir when it pinpointed the earliest known domesticated camels in Palestine much later, around 930 BCE, well after the domestication of the donkey. Their findings, based on an examination of camel bones at an ancient copper smelting–plant in the Aravah Valley, which stretches from the Dead to the Red Sea, would probably not have been global news if it had not contradicted the much earlier appearance of camels in Biblical accounts. The *New York Times* headline from February 10, 2014 read: "Camels had no business in Genesis." Our contemporary Kojak is not the only camel to illuminate human contradictions.

Whether in the Book of Genesis or not, Kojak's predecessors in Jerusalem and other urban environments in Palestine and the wider region have a long and proud history. The recent discovery of a cluster of two-thousand-year-old reliefs and sculptures of camels in a remote site in northern Saudi Arabia attests to the importance, and perhaps veneration, of camels. Writing in the mid-1970s, historian Richard Bulliet claimed camels as major shapers of Arab and Islamic medieval cities. Bulliet mused on why the wheel, so prominent in the carts and chariots of the Roman period in the Middle East, had disappeared in the Islamic period. His answer: camels, particularly tender-footed, preferred sand or dirt to paving stones and shaped the alleys and byways of Arab medieval cities. Many accounts attest to the fact that camels trod the great cities of the region, including the narrow alleys of the Old City of Jerusalem, throughout the nineteenth century. The writer Gustave Flaubert, sitting in a café in the old city of Cairo in 1850, describes the panoply of sound around him, including "camel bells ringing in your ears."

A few traces of the once ubiquitous camel in the city remain in living Jerusalemites' memories. Nazmi Jubeh, a distinguished historian at Birzeit University, was initially surprised by the subject of camels in Jerusalem but then remembered camels delivering heavy goods in the Old City during his boyhood in the 1960s. Fouad Shehadeh, in law school in Jerusalem in the 1940s, at first emphatically said "there were no camels in Jerusalem." But then he recalled camels in the Valley of the Cross, below where the Israel Museum now stands. When a friend kindly assisted me with inquiries about Jerusalem camel memories by emailing relatives who grew up in Jerusalem but were now abroad, one respondent had a rather melancholy Mandate-era memory of a camel "blindfolded and hitched to a millstone, going round and round milling sesame seeds." Issa Boullata, a scholar of Arabic literature, wrote from Canada with a more cheerful account:

> Camels were seen in Jerusalem before 1948. I remember them very well as a boy growing up in the Old City of Jerusalem. They were used to carry heavy loads but were not as common as donkeys. As a boy, I remember a game with other boys: trying to pass to the other side of the road under the rope of a camel being led by its owner through the narrow streets of Jerusalem. One had to be nimble and quick to pass in front of the advancing camel, and not be trodden under. Sometimes there were two camels passing, led by a rope and one had to pass under the rope stretched between the two camels. Funny boyhood games and memories . . .

Camels were also not foreign to Jerusalem's New City, the Western neighborhoods that arose outside the Old City walls in the late nineteenth century and grew rapidly during the British Mandate. An early Mandate-era photo from the Matson Collection, a photo archive dedicated to Palestinian and regional culture and history at the Library of Congress, captioned "View Down Jaffa Road," shows three heavily laden camels alongside a horse-drawn carriage on this main artery from Damascus Gate to the Western neighborhoods. Later in the Mandate, John Rose, the child of an Armenian mother and British father, described how, in his West Jerusalem neighborhood, "Wood was brought around on camelback for heating."

Another striking photo shows gaily adorned camels at Damascus Gate, a handsome entrance to Jerusalem's Old City. Some are kneeling, surrounded by their Bedouin owners. Architect Charles Ashbee, an early civic advisor to the British Mandate, even drew up an unrealized plan for a khan at Damascus Gate to "provide overnight accommodation for the Bedouins and their camels for the purposes of trade." But as the century advanced, Bedouins and their camels were doomed to share the road to Jerusalem with other forms of transport. Late in the Mandate, a model for Damascus Gate prepared by another British planner, Henry Kendall, gives an almost eerie representation of the fate of the camel in Jerusalem: a sole camel and its owner stand by the side of a vast sanitized semicircle with no other sign of human or animal life.

I spoke with Khalil Shawqi, a local Bethlehem historian and architectural conservationist, as we stood overlooking the aptly named Wadi al-Jamal (Valley of Camels) between Bethlehem and Beit Sahur, and he noted that camel herds were stabled in the valley and used to transport produce to Jerusalem until about 1925, when motorized transport began to be used. Camels continued to be used by villagers and Bedouins to get to Jerusalem, he believes, although their numbers in the eponymous valley decreased. An occasional camel still trod the narrow streets of the Old City in the 1960s, but today camel caravans only pace along the alleys of memory.

As camels disappeared in the wake of the 1967 war and the Israeli occupation, one Jerusalem artist transferred the camel's burden to an elderly Arab man in one of the most celebrated of Palestinian images of Jerusalem. In Suleiman Mansour's 1974 painting *Camel of Hardships*, an old, barefoot peasant is bent over with a heavy load; he carries on his back the Old City of Jerusalem, topped by the Dome of the Rock. Reproductions of this painting quickly appeared on T-shirts, postcards, and posters and are still endlessly circulated. The old man is noble but suffering, carrying the burden as well as the beauty of Jerusalem. (As far as I know, no one has ever protested that an elderly man should not be called a camel.) The painting itself has had a strange journey: it was allegedly bought by the young Muammar Gaddafi, the army colonel who ruled Libya, and destroyed in the American bombing of Libya in 1986. In 2005, Mansour was persuaded to re-create the painting, and it was sold at auction by Christie's for a hefty sum.

One of the last camels to bear distant travelers to Jerusalem was the creation of an English novelist. The once-famous opening line of Rose Macaulay's eccentric 1956 travel novel, *The Towers of Trebizond*, reads thus: "'Take my camel, dear,' said my aunt Dot, as she climbed down from this animal on her return from High Mass." The lovelorn first-person narrator responds by taking Aunt Dot's camel, who has inconveniently ended up in England, and traveling with him or her—gender never determined—from Trebizond (Trabzon, on the Black Sea) all the way to Jerusalem. There, she ties up the beast in the garden of Saint George's Anglican Cathedral and hostel, in the heart of East Jerusalem, and incidentally where Raja and I were married.

Kojak, then, had a number of ancestors in the streets of Jerusalem, most real but many, I fear, not remembered, as camels were consigned both in imagination and practice to the desert. What I term "the repressed camel memory syndrome" is particularly prominent among urban Palestinians, as camels came to stand for a primitive mode of life and for countless stereotypes of Arabs in the Western media. The syndrome is made more acute given the efforts to remember the urban society that vanished with the loss of major Palestinian cities in 1948. In the Arab Gulf, for example, no such syndrome is evident, and camel beauty contests continue to celebrate this favorite animal. Indeed, competition is so fierce that owners of twelve camels in the 2018 King Abdulaziz Camel Festival in Saudi Arabia were disqualified for resorting to botox and plastic surgery to enlarge their entries' noses and lips, key features of camel beauty. Camel welfare has also been enhanced by Gulf wealth. In December 2017, a state-of-the-art hospital for camels, costing about eleven million dollars, opened in Dubai. Photos showed the first patients receiving surgery on their sensitive feet.

Palestinians who grew up in Jerusalem, Jaffa, and Haifa during the Mandate may prefer to remember literary societies, excursions in the first automobiles, cinema screenings, or political affiliations rather than beasts of burden with bad breath. The eminent scholar (and scion of a well-known Jerusalem family) Walid Khalidi recently protested to the curator of an exhibit of the work of early Palestinian photographer Khalil Raad: too many camels, he said, asking that some be removed. Khalidi's own important photographic history of the Palestinian people, *Before Their Diaspora*, has a strong focus on urban life in pre-1948 Palestine, with numerous photos of prominent families, major cities, and public events. However, his brief sections on the countryside and rural life contain two revealing photos where camels intrude: in an early twentieth century photo, camels are parked in front of a Muslim religious shrine near Jaffa. In the second, a Mandate-era image, a camel and rider have paused above the Jerusalem-area village of Abu Ghosh. Camels were clearly around in central and coastal Palestine: a personal favorite from the Matson Collection is a 1904 photo of a glamorous wedding camel being readied for a village celebration.

Palestinians with rural upbringings are less reluctant to remember camels. Magid Shihade, who grew up in the Galilee village of Kafr Yasif, recalled his grandfather using camels to plow his fields in the 1950s. Photographer Bassam Almohor, whose family is from a coastal village where Tel Aviv University now stands, grew up as a refugee in the northern West Bank. He recounts stories he heard from his grandfather, who took his camels to Egypt and brought them back laden with goods to sell along the Palestinian coast. Contemporary visual artist Hani Zurob also recalls the stories of his grandfather, who migrated to the coast from his peasant clan in the southern Gaza Strip. At the beginning of the Mandate he bought a camel and struck out for a village near Ramle, where he successfully "transported the village's fruit produce on his camel to the neighboring town markets." In his memoir of growing up in the 1940s on large family farming estates southeast of Gaza, Salman Abu Sitta recalled harvest time, when wheat was piled on the threshing floor to be trampled: "Camels and sometimes oxen pulled the winnowing plate around and around in circles until the thickness of the pile was reduced to a few centimeters." The young Abu Sitta was allowed to sit on the plate, although, he explained ruefully, his weight was not much help.

In Abu Sitta's childhood, camels were familiar denizens of the Palestinian landscape. A 1937 livestock census conducted by the British Mandate counted 72,000 camels in the whole territory of Palestine, which included contemporary Israel. Today, according to 2013 statistics from the Palestinian Central Bureau of Statistics, there are 2,165 camels in Palestine (constituting the West Bank and Gaza), 1,500 in the West Bank (mostly in the southern region) and 680 in Gaza. These are not the only camels between the Mediterranean and the Jordan River. The sweep of camel territory from the southern West Bank to Gaza includes the camels of the Negev (Naqab) Desert, which Israel is responsible to enumerate: according to a recent Israeli estimate, the Negev is the home of another 2,500 camels, a steep decline from the 20,000 found in an informal survey in the early 1990s. We can only hope that camel family reunification lies in the future.

Both British Mandate census officials and our recent camel counters faced similar problems: suspicions from camel owners that their undertaking was for tax purposes. Counting the animals of nomads is impossible, noted one American scholar, Ray Casto, during his stay in Palestine during the Mandate. Today, both in the Palestinian territory and the Negev Desert, Bedouins hesitate to vaccinate their camels for much the same reason, so many remain unregistered and uncounted. The good news is that we can assume camel populations are somewhat higher than the count in both eras; the more disturbing indication, at least for camel advocates, is that many more camels—about fifteen times, at least—inhabited a greater variety of Palestinian landscapes in Mandate times than in the present. Indeed, an Israeli nature site chides gullible tourists for thinking that camels are "running around all over the place," noting that they are found only in the desert or in zoos. With about fifteen million camels living in the Arab region as a whole, there is little fear of the total disappearance of camels, but there is a clear and steep decline in Palestine/Israel, as there is across the river in Jordan, although camels continue to have a ceremonial role in the still-existing Jordan Camel Corps.

The changes in camel population, working histories, and habitat tell us a great deal about the history of the land both camels and humans call home. Where archives and memories fail or fade, photos can help us reconstruct the changing relations between camels and people. Looking through the uncensored lens of the early photographer of Palestine Khalil Raad, we find a fair share of camels posed in biblical landscapes but also hard at work grinding grain in villages, such as Issawiya, near Jerusalem, and delivering goods on narrow streets in Nazareth. A photograph in the Matson Collection shows a long camel train bringing grain from the Dead Sea to Jerusalem in 1917; another image of "Bedouins unloading wheat-laden camels" at Jerusalem's Damascus Gate is dated in the range of 1920–1933.

Camels bearing goods to the Jaffa port also feature in photographs through at least the middle years of the Mandate, as Eyal Sivan's film *Jaffa: The Orange's Clockwork* attests. Jaffa oranges and camels were inseparably linked, as these strong animals carried the heavy crates to the port, perhaps up until the port's closure during the 1936 Arab Revolt and the subsequent opening of a port in Tel Aviv. But as this industry and its markets abroad grew, other forms of transport were needed. Having grown up in the 1940s, Jaffa exile Hassan Hammami does not recall camels working as haulers of oranges but only "seeing camels on rare occasions, and not more than one, two or three, coming into town with some agricultural products, possibly dates from the south." Hammami, the son of an orange exporter, points out that "the amount of oranges grown and exported far exceeded the capacity of any large herd of camels." But Hammami also remembers camel rides as a feature of celebratory fairs during the holidays of Eid al-Adha and Eid al-Fitr at the end of the fasting month of Ramadan, suggesting that the tourist camel had its antecedents. While it is likely that a few camels hauled oranges for smaller enterprises during this period, what is certain is that all that remained after 1948 was the camel as symbol of the Israeli Pardes company, one of the major exporters of "Jaffa oranges." Camels thus metamorphosed into advertising images for the oranges they once carried.

In the crucial three decades of British rule over Palestine, were we simply seeing history roll around again: the camel replacing the wheel and then the inexorable erasure of the camel by the motorized wheel? In the previous centuries of Ottoman rule, the camel had a substantial role in Palestinian agriculture; the Ottoman Land Tax in Palestine exempted "plowing camels," along with other working animals. When British agricultural officials arrived in Palestine, however, they clearly saw it as a ravaged land, and they put the blame firmly on those "rulers of the rural economy," as two officials termed them: camels, sheep, and goats. The first Mandate head of the Department of Agriculture, E. R. Sawer, tellingly described Palestine using the words of a late–nineteenth century clergyman and traveler, George Adam Smith: "The land has been stripped and starved, its bones protrude . . . a carcase of a land."

Palestine had indeed suffered the depredations of World War I, when much of the native forest was felled for fuel for Ottoman troops, but Palestine's "forests" had never resembled any British vision of the forests and fields of home. Armies and human neglect had a much greater environmental effect than nibbling camels. Nonetheless, Britain's attempts to mold Palestine in its own image—as a green and pleasant land—through campaigns against "over-grazing" and for the widespread planting of trees were underwritten by a distinctly sour view of both camels and their Bedouin owners. When the British left in 1948 the landscapes they left behind in the hills of the Galilee and the Mediterranean coast had lost much of their Bedouin population, along with their companion animals. And the new state of Israel had little room for Bedouins and thus for camels, except as picturesque—and manageable—icons of the past.

The story of working camels in Mandate-era Palestinian agriculture was shaped not only by British policies but by the growing conflict between the Zionist movement (with its flood of new immigrants from Europe) and Palestinians, particularly peasants. Most salient was the increasing dispossession and landlessness of tenant peasants (*fellahin* in Arabic), as land purchases by Zionist organizations—often from urban-based Arab landowners—increased. Nonetheless, agriculture remained at the center of the Palestinian economy throughout this period, employing 53 percent of the settled population, according to the 1930 census—a population overwhelmingly Arab at 93 percent. This figure did not include the unsettled Bedouins and their flocks of goats and camels.

Palestinian peasants raised sheep and goats for milk and meat while camels, along with mules and donkeys, were used as working animals and for transport, as Israeli researcher Roza El-Eini has noted. Casto, who has a keen eye (and perhaps orientalist-tinted glasses) for camels, gives them a central role in olive oil production in this period, replacing humans in the laborious work of extracting oil: "Today the stone [the millstone] is turned by an animal, usually a camel blindfolded so that it will not grow dizzy, harnessed to the stone by a long pole."

Despite the centrality of these working animals, as well as their flocks of sheep and goats, to peasant and Bedouin welfare, British officials saw them as enemies. In particular, the "unsettled Bedouin" and their cross-border grazing of herds of camels, goats, and sheep were the subject of a number of acts of Mandate legislation. As Ghazi Falah points out in his study of the Galilee Bedouin, the aim was to halt Bedouin mobility across the Palestinian landscape and settle them in permanent locations. The British attempt to govern and mold Bedouin tribes culminated in the draconian Bedouin Control Ordinance No. 18 of 1942, which granted district commissioners the power to "exercise general control and supervision over all or any nomadic tribes or tribesmen, superintend their movements and wherever he considers it necessary to direct them to go, or not to go, or to remain in any special area for any specific period." That the movement of Bedouin populations was generally south—to Bir Saba (Beersheba), the Negev (Naqab) Desert, and what the British called the "hot and unclaimed areas of the Jordan Valley"—is surely part of the explanation for the vanishing of camels from other Palestinian landscapes.

Not every British official agreed with these policies, and conflicts arose. In the 1940s, the Jerusalem district commissioner noted that each spring, Bedouins drove a large number of camels from Beersheba to the Jericho area, seeking pasturage, and proposed that a reserve in Jericho be open for grazing. Gilbert Sale, the head of the Department of Forestry, objected. The commissioner then argued that "an Arab will go a long way actually and metaphysically to save the life of his camel," and warned against "a lack of sympathy." El-Eini gives the succinct reply of Sale, who was determined to hold onto a 321-acre forest area near Jericho: "The attitudes of the forester towards his trees closely resembles that of the Arab towards his camel."

Given the constellation of forces, the forester won this battle. Camels were not only consigned to the desert but—like their Arab owners—were increasingly configured as primitive and contrasted with an emerging modernity. A popular Mandate-era postcard (which still turns up as a vintage item on eBay) shows a camel with its Arab owner, traveling alongside a truck and a modern train.

But during the political turmoil and economic trans-formation of the first half of the twentieth century, the camel entered and exited with a bang. Camels were not only working animals in the fields, orchards, and villages of Palestine; they were literally fellow combatants, including in one of the first clashes between Palestinian villagers and Zionist settlers in 1913 when Palestine was still part of the Ottoman Empire. In the account of Jewish immigrants from the new coastal settlement of Rishon Letzion, Arab "thugs" from the nearby village of Zarnuqa on "heavily loaded camels" stole grapes from settlement vineyards and beat up a Jewish guard. The ensuing conflict left two Jews and one Arab dead. An Israeli scholar, Yuval Ben-Bassat, reviewing petitions by Palestinians to the Ottoman Sultan in the Istanbul Archives, discovered an alternative story. In a petition by heads of Arab families in the village to Sultan Mehmet V in Istanbul, the villagers complained to the Sultan that the Jewish settlers "wanted to strip the camel owners of their clothes, money and camels." The peasants refused to give up their camels and escaped, but then, the petitioners told the Sultan, "the above mentioned Jews attacked our villages, robbed and looted our property, killed and even damaged the family honor, all this in a manner we find hard to put into words." And indeed, their words were not heard for more than a century, until a diligent scholar rescued them from an Ottoman archive.

Ben-Bassat's account gives us a glimpse of camels as valuable working animals in coastal Palestine and also of camels embroiled in human antagonisms. It was not the first time and it would not be the last. During an earlier conflict, monks in Jerusalem's Old City made a highly innovative use of camels. In 1853, the Crimean War broke out after the Ottoman Sultan gave concessions in Jerusalem to Catholic France rather than to Orthodox Russia. Russia promptly declared war on the Ottomans and their allies Britain and France. Doing their bit for the war effort, Orthodox monks in wartime Jerusalem herded camels into the residence of the newly appointed Catholic patriarch, a less deadly, although perhaps more smelly, form of political–religious clash than we witness in the present.

One of history's oddest incidents of camels in warfare, however, occurred around the same time but an ocean away. In the mid-nineteenth century, camels were returned from the Arab region to the western plains of the United States that their camelid ancestors had inhabited ten million years ago. Officers in the American cavalry, in their wisdom, had decided camels were just the mount needed in the fight against Native American tribes in the arid and expanding western territories. Seventy-seven camels in two shipments landed at Anatolia, Texas, accompanied by a Syrian camel caretaker called Hadji Ali, whose name was quickly changed by American soldiers to Hi Jolly. Hi Jolly could not be everywhere to counter the army's almost complete ignorance of camel behavior. Camels reportedly happily ate the acacia fence in which they were penned, and soldiers suffered camel bites along with the famous sideways kicks.

The camels nonetheless proved their worth on a grueling surveying expedition, leading to a commendation in a US congressional report. The eruption of the Civil War ended the army's camel experiment, and the animals were either sold or let loose in the western deserts, where accounts of feral camel sightings, including the famous and feared Red Ghost, continued for decades. The official account from an army history website ends with a note of regret for the camels' demise: "Ignored and abandoned, it was an ignominious and unfortunate end for these noble 'ships of the desert.'"

Hadji Ali, as Hi Jolly, fared only slightly better than his camel companions. He remained in the United States, marrying a woman named Gertrude in Tucson. Three years later, he wandered back to the hills with a few camels and resumed life as a desert prospector. When he returned home in failure, Gertrude refused to take him back, and he seems to have become the resident, and only, Imam of a makeshift mosque in Tucson. He is commemorated by a camel-topped monument in Quartzsite, Arizona.

The camel at war in the Middle East is perhaps most famously associated with World War I and the Arab Revolt, when Sharif Hussein bin Ali of the Hejaz, encouraged and supported by the British, mobilized Arab tribes to rebel against the Ottomans. The British icon of the revolt was indubitably Lawrence of Arabia (T. E. Lawrence), who once requested two thousand camels from his British superior. Unlike many Western travelers, Lawrence had a sympathetic affinity for camels: he criticized the British Imperial Camel Corps for overloading their animals, although in his excitement during the successful raid on the Ottoman garrison at Aqaba he shot his own camel in the head. Camels were among the many victims in the Great War in Palestine: Inchbald described the endless line of camel corpses on the road from Jaffa to Jerusalem when the Camel Corps was deployed as "Allenby's bluff," a decoy to lure the

Ottoman troops away from the main British force that attacked, and eventually conquered, Jerusalem in December 1917.

In wartime Jerusalem, Djemal Pasha, supreme commander of the Fourth Ottoman Army, was always protected by a camel-mounted squadron of guards. One suspects that camels featured prominently in his entrance into the city in November 1914, although his departure by train in 1917 was camel-less and lackluster. When the British Imperial Camel Corps—which also fought in Gaza and Beersheba in October 1917—was disbanded before the end of World War I, primarily to free troops for the Western Front, it did not mark the definitive end of camel participation in human conflict and diplomacy. Several years later, an Egyptian camel bucked British Colonial Secretary Winston Churchill as he attempted to force its pace during a ride to the Great Pyramids in 1921. His fall came at the conclusion of the Cairo conference, which resulted in Churchill boasting that he created the Kingdom of Jordan "with one stroke of the pen, one Sunday morning in Cairo." Legend has it that Churchill was inebriated at the time, hence a zigzag along the eastern border with Saudi Arabia that is still called "Winston's hiccup."

As the Mandate commenced in Palestine, the camel was also mobilized for purposes of "public order." An interim report of the British Civil Administration, which prior to the British Mandatory government ruled Palestine for a year, addressed questions of civil obedience and security and noted the establishment of a new gendarmerie, including thirty men mounted on camels. This "highly trained" force, better paid than the Palestine Police, would be deployed in the protection of frontiers and the suppression of internal disturbances. Mounted camels suppressing internal disturbances rings a contemporary bell, as we recall the vicious attack on demonstrators in Cairo's Tahrir Square on February 2, 2011, by camel and horse riders who had been mobilized to support President Hosni Mubarak. A century earlier, it is more likely that these camel-riding British gendarmes were directed against Bedouins and their camels, then present in numerous locations in Palestine, including the Galilee and the coastal plains, and whose movements across the new borders—imaginary lines entirely unrecognized by Bedouins— were viewed suspiciously.

It is an ironic reversal that the last glimpse we have of camels at war is when Palestinians used them against the British. In 1936, Palestine erupted in the Great Revolt. Launched with a general strike, the revolt was fuelled by the continuing dispossession of peasants from their land, and many took to the hills and formed guerilla bands, confronting the British security services. As the revolt raged on, one-third of the British army was deployed in Palestine. In December 1937, Charles Tegart, a colonial police officer in Calcutta with a long experience of "putting down" Indian insurgencies, was summoned to advise. Along with a series of forts across the country, he recommended building a barrier fence between Palestine and Lebanon. It was termed by *Time* magazine, in an eerie precursor of contemporary headlines, "Britain's most ingenious solution for handling terrorism in Palestine." The fence barred many civilians from access to their farmland and blocked their freedom of movement, but it proved no impediment to the rebels. A scholar of security studies, Laleh Khalili, explained: "The Arabs dragged it apart with camels."

While camels have been largely absent from more recent conflicts in Palestine and Israel, their cousins from South America have only just retired from a long period of service in the Israeli army. Llamas, who, like camels, are descendants of the camelids of North America, were used by the Israeli army to carry equipment in several wars, including the 2006

Lebanon War. Soldiers then ungratefully complained that the slow-paced llamas held them back. The llamas were decommissioned in September 2017, to be replaced, like many workers around the world, by robots.

Walking in the Jerusalem wilderness in February 2017, the hills lightly coated with spring green, we arrived at the shrine of Nebi Musa, the tomb of Moses, its whitewashed domes gleaming in the sunlight. Greeting us was a young frisky camel. When we fed him an apple, his owner quickly renamed him Touffah, the Arabic word for apple. Our fellow walkers, Gerard and Salwa, were entranced when the camel owner told them that he guided trips on Touffah all the way from Nebi Musa to Mar Saba, the monastery perched high on the cliffs above a long wadi from the Dead Sea. A few weeks later, on March 8, International Women's Day, Gerard decided to treat Salwa to a ride. Touffah by then had been renamed Fustu (peanut), and Salwa described the eight-hour ride up the steep and stony way: "I have never been more uncomfortable. Everything hurt." What Fustu thought of carrying his unhappy feminist rider remains unknown.

Pressure on the Jerusalem municipality from Israeli tour guides eventually secured Kojak's release from his dark prison, after a Tel Aviv insurance company agreed to insure its first-ever camel. However, it was not a happy ending for Kojak, as Raja and I discovered when we sought out Mr. Abu Hawa on the Mount of Olives. On that clear sunny day in December 2012, a lively looking camel stood in the light breeze with Mr. Abu Hawa sitting beside him. But alas, although he was named Kojak, he was not the former prisoner, as Abu Hawa explained angrily. When the first Kojak was taken, a "racist doctor" said he needed a shot, and Mr. Abu Hawa briskly answered: "*You* need a shot." Kojak was detained for twenty days. When he was finally released, he emitted a loud and terrible groan—Abu Hawa attempted an imitation—and attacked his owner. Kojak had become *majnun* (crazed) during his incarceration. Although he was put out to pasture, the traumatized Kojak today prefers to hunker down by himself in a dark place. The new Kojak is only eight years old and should have a long career ahead of him, as camels live for three to four decades, but Abu Hawa is not optimistic. "No animals in Jerusalem," he says, summing up municipal policy. The new Kojak has a license today, but his future is not secure.

We drove back to Ramallah from Jerusalem along the Separation Wall, which Palestinians call the Apartheid Wall. This stretch of the Wall in East Jerusalem separates Palestinian neighborhood from Palestinian neighborhood and is thus better named, as Amaney, a young Palestinian activist from Grassroots Jerusalem argues, the "isolation wall." I recalled the crucial role of camels in pulling down the Tegart wall in Mandate Palestine. I imagined these "primitive" camels riding again, high above in the current fragmented and degraded urban landscape of Jerusalem, ready to pull down another Wall.

CHAPTER 2

MAMMALS BEHAVING BADLY: HYENAS, HUMANS, AND TALES OF FEAR AND LOATHING

Abu Hassan, a striped hyena, sleepily raises his head and looks at me. His pointy ears seem too large for him, which I find endearing. Abu Hassan is lying at the back of his cage, a resident of the West Bank's only zoo, in the town of Qalqilya. Although it is only an hour away from Ramallah, where I live, neither I nor my three (somewhat reluctant) companions have visited Qalqilya in many years. Located on the "border" with Israel proper and just seven and a half miles from the Mediterranean Sea, the town is sealed on three sides; the only access is through a military checkpoint that is manned, off and on, by one or two bored Israeli soldiers. In better days, West Bank residents and Palestinian and Jewish shoppers from inside Israel mingled during visits to Qalqilya, a town famed for its inexpensive second-hand furniture, culled from nearby and more prosperous Israeli towns, and its excellent humus and falafel. Nowadays, we visit a zoo with animals behind bars in a city that is likewise imprisoned.

Zoos, even the best of them, are uneasy places. John Berger has observed that public zoos came into existence in Europe and the United States when animals were vanishing from daily life, calling zoos an "epitaph to a relationship which was as old

Abu Hassan, six years old, at Qalqilya Zoo, July 2018.
(Credit: Bassam Almohor)

as man." My worries were less sweeping as we paid the small entrance fee at the Qalqilya zoo; I simply feared that our Palestinian zoo would be run-down, with animals languishing in miserable conditions. But the zoo, with pleasant picnic areas and shady trees, was full of enthusiastic local visitors, including what must have been a sizeable portion of the local Palestinian police and security personnel on holiday, taking selfies in front of the more impressive animals. The hippopotamus drew an especially large crowd and was a favorite for photos. Uniformed police officers and kids alike then gravitated to an open-air meeting honoring Palestinian children imprisoned by Israel. The tone over the loudspeaker as a woman celebrates her fifteen-year-old son's release from detention was more cheerful than strident. The audience clapped and whistled, an outing Palestinian style.

The children then beetled toward a nearby cage with two weary-looking lions, the most melancholy of the zoo's animals, most of whom were residing in much better conditions than I had expected. Abu Hassan does not garner much attention except from me, as I am among the very few fans of the *Hyaena hyaena*, the smaller and shyer cousin of the spotted hyena that is found in much of sub-Saharan Africa. The striped hyena has a large but patchy range from East Africa through the Middle East to India. It has inhabited Palestine, its deserts, valleys, and hills, for thousands of years.

But it is the striking tales of fear and loathing that its human neighbors in Palestine have told of this ever-present but rarely glimpsed mammal that have piqued my curiosity about hyenas and their elusive lives in the Palestinian landscape. Even casual visitors to lands inhabited by hyenas seem to go out of their way to cast aspersions on this intelligent, if ungainly, creature. In 1904, US President Theodore Roosevelt, whose personal menagerie featured a small bear and a one-legged rooster, received a spotted hyena named Bill as a present from the Emperor Menelik II of Abyssinia (Ethiopia). This thoughtful gift did not soften Roosevelt's acerbic tone when he went on safari in 1909 and described the hyena thus:

> "in all my associations with hunters, travelers, and naturalists I have never yet been able to find one who would defend the hyena, which by common consent is classed as the most skulking, cowardly, cruel and treacherous of beasts.

Uncertain that I am qualified to be the sole defender of this much-maligned mammal, I proceed to visit the chief and only vet at the zoo, Dr. Sami Khader. We meet in his office, crowded not only with papers, coffee cups, and mysterious vials but with a small baby baboon playing under Dr. Sami's feet. Loozeh (Arabic for almond) was born in the spring when the almond trees were blossoming but was roundly rejected by her mother, who promptly tried to kill her. As Dr. Sami's long-suffering wife has refused any more animals at home, Loozeh has been doing her bit to add to office chaos.

I try to concentrate and hear Abu Hassan's story. Dr. Sami explains that he was called to the scene when Abu Hassan's front paw was caught in a trap near Ramallah several years ago. The hunter was too frightened of the hunted animal to release him. Fear circulates, and I wonder for a moment whether the occupier's fear of the occupied keeps us all captive. But why such fear of an injured hyena?

"I don't take animals from the wild," Dr. Sami explained. "It's not right and I don't want to encourage a black market." But Abu Hassan could no longer roam the hills and wadis favored by the diminishing hyena population. Like more than half of the large mammals (megafauna) around the globe threatened with extinction due chiefly to habitat loss, striped hyenas have followed the downward trajectory from common animal a century ago to nearly threatened in the last decades to endangered today. Dr. Sami took Abu Hassan back to the zoo but had to amputate his paw.

A valiant protector of his zoo animals, Dr. Sami has been obliged nonetheless to teach himself taxidermy to stuff those of his wards who perished during various Israeli military curfews and incursions into his town, which kept animals from getting food and the attention they needed. The most catastrophic event was the Israeli army's invasion during the spring of 2002 in the wake of a Palestinian suicide bombing in the coastal town of Netanya. As Israeli soldiers advanced into Qalqilya accompanied by gunshots and explosions, Brownie, a male giraffe, was literally frightened to death, slamming his head into the metal doorway of his cage. Refusing to eat, his pregnant mate Ruti delivered a stillborn calf a week after Brownie's sad demise. With daily visits and treats from Dr. Sami, Ruti gradually seemed to recover, but when she died five years later, one of the staff told Dr. Sami "She died of a broken heart." The pair of giraffes are featured, stuffed by Dr. Sami, in the zoo's rather eccentric museum, along with less famous victims of long curfews, such as stuffed owls on a perch (who starved to death). Both Brownie and Ruti had found their way to the Qalqilya zoo thanks to Dr. Sami's longstanding relationship with an Israeli colleague at the Tel Aviv zoo, who dispatched the pair with some difficulty to the beleaguered town. It is a cooperation that whispers across an increasingly unbridgeable divide, solidarity between animal lovers.

I return to Abu Hassan's cage and stand on the rail. My

attempts to convince my companion Susan that he is not ugly meet with little success. With a sloping back, an ungainly head with a large muzzle, prominent teeth (suitable for bone crushing), and a zig zag walk, the hyena is not the most graceful of the large mammals in Palestine. And scavengers, despite their important ecological niche, rarely excite human affection. In Palestine and elsewhere, the hyena is stigmatized by persistent stories of his sinister penchant for robbing graves. The unpleasant (to humans) way that hyenas mark their territory with powerful odors from their anal glands is also not particularly engaging. And their preternatural giggle at night is sometimes mentioned with a shiver, although oddly it is the larger spotted hyena of Africa that mainly sounds this call, not our quieter striped version. Growing up in 1950s Jerusalem, my historian colleague Musa was convinced he heard hyenas in the narrow strip of No Man's Land between East and West Jerusalem, while I am almost certain he heard the cries of jackals, which still sound in the Jerusalem night. But nasty giggles, foul smells, and a penchant for graves, whether real or rumored, can't account entirely for the visceral human antagonism that hyenas evoke.

I begin to piece together the evidence for and against the elusive hyena. My only previous encounter with a hyena was a stuffed and sorry-looking specimen standing in a dimly lit glass vitrine in Jerusalem's Natural History Museum, an attractive stone building built by an Armenian businessman as a private home in 1862. Since then, it has housed the Ottoman governor of Jerusalem, the British High Commissioner, and a British officer's club, before its incarnation as a rather run-down museum. The hyena, with a few rocks scattered around him to suggest a desert setting, seemed a relic from another time, perhaps prepared for exhibition after he was hunted and killed by an English Mandatory officer relaxing from policing the unruly population, both Arabs and Jews. Thought-provoking in a different vein were two photographs I found in a Library of Congress collection covering the early days of the Tel Aviv zoo, sometime in the 1930s. Both feature a young Jewish zookeeper, in a trim wool vest, and a furry young striped hyena. The hyena's cage is open. In one image, the keeper leans down to give the hyena a treat; in another, the hyena stands on his hind legs to nuzzle the keeper's chest in a clear gesture of affection. The relation is intriguing because it is so unusual: Can hyenas become fond of humans and vice versa? A mural from Egypt's Old Kingdom (2750 BCE) shows a man shepherding a young striped hyena, one of the few clues that hyenas might have had a brief period of domestication. A stone relief from the same period suggests the reason: a hyena on its back is being fattened with a goose or duck for a tasty meal. Neither suggests the relation between the 1930s zookeeper and the kept hyena. Perhaps hyenas, absent from northern Europe since the last interglacial age, did not haunt the imagination of this new European immigrant to Palestine as they did the native inhabitants.

This seldom-seen scavenger, however, is very much present in Palestinian imaginations—with contemporary conditions sometimes adding a nightmarish edge. In a 2007 documentary film, *The Dream of the Hyena*, posted on the site Palestine Calling, a Palestinian from Hebron faces the camera and recounts a dream he had while enduring miserable conditions in an Israeli desert prison during the First Palestinian Intifada (1987–1993), a time of mass detention of Palestinian protestors. In the dream, his father is telling him the story of Abu Yusef. Pursued by a hyena, the beleaguered and inept Abu Yusef finds a match to ward off the beast but fails to light it in time and is eviscerated and devoured. Abu Yusef, under many names and with various fates (sometimes he escapes), has been encountering the hypnotic hyena in folk tales over the centuries, but in this account the moral has a twist. "And then I understood what my father was telling me," said the ex-prisoner. "Fear and despair are the hyena."

It is the fear of this timid beast that most intrigues me. "Come home before dark or the hyenas will eat you": my friend Jamil, now an eminent sociologist, recalled his mother's constant refrain when he was a young boy tending his family's flock on the edge of the Jerusalem wilderness. Her warning is embedded in tale after tale of hyenas in Palestinian folklore, which often add the eerie fantastical ability of the hyena to paralyze his victim with his hypnotic stare—perhaps derived from the gleaming eyes of this nocturnal creature—before devouring his unfortunate prey.

Simon Awad is the director of the Environmental Education Center, housed at the Talitha Kumi Lutheran School in the southern West Bank town of Beit Jala. A slight man with a ready smile, Simon is one of a new generation of Palestinian environmental activists. On the school's pleasant hilltop campus, he and his staff have founded a thriving bird-monitoring and ringing station and a new initiative to track mammals as well. Busloads of schoolchildren visit the Center each week for talks and for strolls on the rope bridges erected among the tall cypresses and flowering plants.

Awad is a passionate defender of the hyena and other endangered animals in Palestine. However, he recalls his grandmother warning him as a child about the "magical sparks" from a hyena's eyes: "A bride was hypnotized by a hyena after looking directly into its eyes," she told the young boy. "This drove her to follow the hyena to its cave where she was killed and eaten."

His grandmother's story lingered in Simon's adult imagination when he had his own encounter with the sad effects of hyena hysteria on a summer night in 2007.

Simon was coming home from the exhausting ordeal of crossing the bridge from Jordan into the West Bank when he received a phone call. An employee at the Center reported an injured hyena in the small forest below Beit Jala: "Ghazi told me that I might have trouble from some young men if I tried to rescue the animal," Simon told me. "So I took two boy scouts who were camping at the Center along with me. When I arrived, the hyena was already dead."

The hyena had been shot, although the young men from Beit Safafa, a suburban Arab neighborhood on the southern edge of Jerusalem, claimed he had been hit by a car. "They were drunk," Simon said flatly, "and they said they would give me the hyena if I bought them a case of beer. I refused." The two hefty boy scouts accompanying Simon would not pick up the hyena, fearing he might come back to life. So Simon raised the corpse by the ears and had a strange experience: he, too, felt a shiver of fear that the hyena might open his eyes. "Culture is stronger than science, " he concluded ruefully. Today, the stuffed hyena is an exhibit in the Center's small museum, along with a companion hyena who was shot by a monk in the desert monastery of Mar Saba, below Bethlehem. Hyenas, it seems, are safe from no one.

It is a difficult mission to fight such deep-seated fear and revulsion. Tales of treacherous hyenas abound in Palestinian, Arab, African, and Indian folklore, constituting what might be called a world-historical bad press. Oddly, though the hyena is so widely feared, it is also seen almost universally as cowardly. In school at the House of Orphans in Jerusalem's Old City during the British Mandate, Reja-e Busailah relished a fellow student's referring to Richard the Lionheart, defeated by Saladin, as Richard the Hyena-Heart. Whether as eaters of corpses, skulking cowards, or magical creatures with hypnotic eyes, this "unattractive creature," as one Israeli anthropologist studying hyena lore among the Bedouin termed his subject, is seen positively only in its parts. For example, in the early twentieth century, residents of the Palestinian town of Hebron consumed hyena meat as a cure for fever, and hyena paws in India sometimes are used as talismans. The longstanding dispute over whether hyenas are more closely related to dogs or cats (or the catlike mongoose) has been partly resolved by placing them in their own unique family, the *Hyaenidae*. No one seems to want the hyena.

Given the hyena's reputation, the hunter of this unsightly carnivore has sought ways to protect himself from his prey. Consider an unusual method deployed by hunters in the vanished village of Al-Bassa in the Upper Galilee, a forested region cut by long ravines and dotted with caves hospitable to hyenas. Before most of its inhabitants were forced to flee in the 1948 war, Al-Bassa was a prosperous farming village, boasting an elementary school, two churches, two mosques, and a mixed population of about three thousand Christian and Muslim Arabs. Such religious cohabitation was not unusual in historic Palestine, but Al-Bassa, according to the memoirs of the noted economist Yusif Sayigh, who grew up in the village, had a special character. "People drank a huge amount, not just the Christians but the Moslems, and gambled a great deal and smuggled a great deal," Yusif recalled, also noting a marked tolerance among villagers for adulterous women and a fondness for scandalous gossip and plays translated into Arabic from the French. Bassawis (residents of Al-Bassa) also had a bent for striking storytelling, as in this account from a Palestinian refugee in Lebanon on how to hunt a hyena, called by the Bassawis "Abu Sirhan":

> The traditional Bassawi way of hunting the hyena was rather strange. They used to say that only the brave ones with a heart as strong as a rock could do it. That way of hunting used to start by trapping the hyena in a cave by throwing stones at it to prevent it from coming out or running away. The hunter would then strip naked and crawl backwards on all fours, through the tunnels leading to the inside of the cave while saying *"Abu Sirhan hon? La' mish hon."* (Is Abu Sirhan here? No he is not here). Of course the hyena would not see a face: it would only hear a sound coming out of an unusual-looking creature with no head crawling towards it. They used to say that the hyena would get so frightened, that it would stick to the back wall of the cave almost totally paralyzed. Then the hunter used to put the *lijam* (mouth cover) on the hyena and bind it. When that was done, the hunter would drag it out of the cave and kill it.

When the Bassawi hunters exposed their private parts to bewildered hyenas, they were engaging with a familiar creature in the Palestinian landscape. Henry Tristram, documenting Palestine's flora and fauna in the late nineteenth century for the Palestine Exploration Fund, observed: "The Hyena is common in every part of Palestine and indifferent as to the character of the country. The old rock-hewn tombs and innumerable caves afford it convenient cover. Its wail may always be heard at nightfall. It attacks graves and burrows into them, even in the vicinity of towns. It is mentioned once in the Scriptures, but translated 'speckled bird.'"

Raja and I recently took a long walk in one of the most beautiful Israeli nature reserves in the Upper Galilee. We followed a path along the Amud Stream, which flows through a deep ravine and whose banks are dotted with lemon and pomegranate trees, most planted before 1948 by the now-absent Arab inhabitants of the hilltop town of Safed. At the trailhead, a sign displayed sketches of the mammals which a fortunate visitor might encounter. To my delight, a delicate sketch of a hyena looking rather hungrily at a tortoise was among them. As we crossed a bridge over a spring-fed pond surrounded by Oriental plane trees, we met three of the reserve staff resting from repairing a path. My few words of Hebrew do not include hyena, so I asked hopefully in English, "Have you ever seen signs of a hyena?" One looked puzzled and then said no, there were no hyenas. The second offered a consolation prize: at night, he told us, he often hears the sounds of weasels. The third corrected his colleague's English: "He meant jackals." Agreeing that jackals are common, I moved on, disconsolate. The reserve is not that far from the site where Al-Bassa once stood and where hyenas were common enough that hunters regularly had to drop their pants to deceive them.

Today, the striped hyena is classified as endangered in Israel and near-threatened in other sites in the Middle East and India. The sole Palestinian biodiversity study, undertaken in 1999, estimated their number in the West Bank at only two hundred. A slightly more cheerful figure of three to five hundred was offered by Imad Atrash of the Palestine Wildlife Society in 2015, although he also feared their extinction. In a recent conversation, he reverted to the estimate of two hundred. Scientists at the Islamic University of Gaza declared the hyena extinct in Gaza in 2007. However, since few large mammals are indigenous to Gaza, any hyena spotted there earlier may well have been a migrating visitor from the Naqab (Negev) Desert. At present, Israel's electronic fence along its "border" with Gaza—begun in 1994 and now firmly in place with underground barriers to prevent tunneling—deters animal as well as human circulation. In 2003, however, a wolf and two jackals managed to find their way through a gap in the fence. None of the trio survived for long in Gaza.

Given the hyena's precarious existence, why does this vanishing animal continue to evoke fear? One young American anthropologist proposed an answer from our evolutionary history. Marcus Baynes-Rock spent several years observing spotted hyenas in the Ethiopian city of Harar, one of the few sites where hyenas have a sacred status and a companionable existence with humans. He wondered why hyenas are so loathed elsewhere. His answer was ingenious if not provable: hyenas are our old enemy, he asserts, who crunched our diminutive bipedal ancestors when we came down from the African trees. As we became "more human by acting like hyenas," we competed with hyenas for the leftover kill of lions, "establishing sour relations with hyenas for millions of years to come."

My environmentalist friend Simon Awad has a region-specific explanation for the tensions between locals and hyenas. During World War I, he observed correctly, many Arab conscripts tried to flee the Ottoman army. "What the Turkish soldiers would do to prevent this was take conscripts into the hills and show them skulls, saying 'That is what the hyena will do to you if you run away.'" Prominent historian Sami Hadawi's memoir of his childhood during World War I provides us with additional insight. As hunger and disease raged in Jerusalem in the spring of 1916, Hadawi's mother gathered her family into a carriage for a night flight from Jerusalem to Jericho. She told the awed children the next morning that a hyena had visited them in the night and "stood up on its hind legs and attempted to get in the carriage." Hadawi attributed the "infestation of hyenas" in the area—note the language of pestilence—to the many carcasses of dead horses and camels left behind by Turkish troops, a rich feast for hungry scavengers. The skulls the hyenas left behind were thus conveniently available to Ottoman commanders to frighten gullible Palestinian conscripts. To this day, a long valley from the Jerusalem wilderness to Jericho is called the Valley of the Hyenas.

Almost a century later, villagers in the Hebron region in the southern West Bank complained of another "infestation of hyenas." In December 2010, they appealed to the Palestinian police to assist "with a recent expansion of the hyena population," citing threats to dogs, livestock, and children. The police responded that they could not intervene because they needed authorization from the Israeli police: the villagers had the misfortune to reside outside Area A, the 18 percent of the West Bank where Palestinian police can operate relatively freely, according to the Oslo Accords.

A researcher from Palestine Polytechnic University in nearby Hebron, Imadeddin Albaba, used cameras in various locations in the West Bank for a period of fifteen months (April 2014–August 2015) to track and chart the hyena population. The traps revealed only one image—a male hyena marking his territory with urine near the Wadi Al-Quff forest reserve in the southern West Bank. In the previous five years, Albaba also notes, the Palestinian press carried at least ten accounts of hyena sightings, but all of them resulting in the killing of the hyena.

Could the lack of protection for Palestinians living in the fragmented rural landscape of contemporary Palestine translate into fear of a nocturnal scavenger? Hyenas generally eat only carrion, with an occasional porcupine or piece of fruit as an aperitif. The Hebron area villagers' sole reported loss was a dead cow, and there was no clear evidence to suggest the cow's demise was due to a hyena. Nonetheless, villagers said they were afraid to leave their homes in the dark, a signal that fear of hyenas goes well beyond actual dangers, and that old fears of the hyena have been married to new insecurities.

Simon Awad has investigated every story he hears of hyenas attacking domestic animals or threatening children and found no evidence. Hyena specialist Omar Attum, a wildlife biologist from Indiana University Southeast who works across the river in Jordan, concurs. When I wrote him, he also confirmed that hyenas are not dangerous, adding that he can find no recorded evidence of hyena attacks on livestock or humans. In his investigation, Omar and his dedicated team disguised themselves as trees to observe hyenas for several weeks in Jordan's Wadi Dana.

Nonetheless, the hated scavenger is an unwelcome neighbor in Palestine and even if scarce, may be coming closer to its reluctant human companions. It is highly likely that hyenas are more frequently sighted near human habitation because of the Israeli-built Separation Wall. The Wall, Awad and a host of environmentalists attest, has caused ecological fragmentation, both of flora and of fauna, and in particular has disrupted animal circulation for food and mating, raising fears of genetic isolation. Environmental lobbyists in Israel had successfully lobbied for several "zigzag passages" for smaller animals, but large mammals share the fate of humans, although without the intricate permit system that governs Palestinian life. Hyenas and other large mammals are thus forced into more human contact and encounter more human hostility.

Awad understands people's fear of hyenas: he experienced it

himself when confronted with the corpse of a hyena on a summer night. His grandmother not only told him tales of hyenas but shooed him out of her house, saying "go home early, there are hyenas." But he hopes environmental education might teach a younger generation to overcome their fear not only of hyenas but of other animals that rouse ancient suspicions. "People still kill owls," he says sadly, "because they think they are very bad luck." When I asked Simon if he had heard of any recent hyena sightings, he said there was one in the Hebron district in late 2015, where a hyena was killed. "You can find it on YouTube," he said softly and left it there.

When I opened one of several video postings of this incident, I saw why Simon looked so pained. A hyena, his head down, is running along the verge of a road in the daytime. This is such unusual behavior for a shy nocturnal animal that avoids exposure that it is almost impossible not to link it to shrinking habitat, either because of the Wall or from other changes in the built environment. He is followed by a group of young Palestinian men in a car who are throwing stones at him. An unseen photographer in another car is filming. The hyena stops and cowers. The young men get out of the car and kill him with a blow to the head. Several vehicles with young male passengers gather at the scene. The killing of the hyena, which I can hardly watch, is the opposite of a furtive act. It is a public act, displayed with some pride. Young males have destroyed hyenas out of fear or anger for centuries—it is a winter rite of passage in some Lebanese mountain villages. In colonial India, young British officers on horseback killed hyenas for sport in a cruel version of polo. But forcing myself to watch the video a second time, I recognized something familiar in the collective action of these hyena hunters. Young men (and indeed young women) in Palestine—collectively called the *shebab*—have been on the front lines in defending their families, communities, and universities against the Israeli army, perhaps most famously in the First Palestinian Intifada, where they were termed the "children of stones," after the only weapon they possessed. Recalling the fruitless appeals of Hebron-area villagers for police protection from hyenas, I consider whether the young men who stoned this defenseless hyena also saw themselves as protectors of their villages, as well as being motivated by the fear absorbed from their mothers' and grandmothers' warnings of the hyena's hypnotic powers.

I looked at other sites that had posted the same video. An Israeli site displayed the headline: "Hyena Heartlessly Stoned to Death by 'Palestinian' Arabs." The quotation marks around "Palestinian" are meant to signal that Palestinians do not exist as a people, a trope used frequently by right-wing Israelis. A brutal death of an animal is used to discount a people: it is no wonder that many Palestinians, even those concerned with the environment and animal welfare, are cynical about Israeli environmentalists advocating passage for animals, but not Palestinians, through the Separation Wall. The dilemma for those who consider that human and animal welfare are intertwined is very real. Ibrahim Odeh, a spokesman for the Palestine Wildlife Society, called the killing of the hyena in Hebron "murder," adding that the lack of a Palestinian law protecting wildlife gave the "public a free hand to handle such a precious species mercilessly." Strong words, indeed, but his condemnation appeared only in a newspaper in the distant Gulf.

Imad Atrash told me a more heartening story. In the same year that the Hebron-area hyena met his death, Imad found a hyena in a trap near the nature center the society has established at Auja, an oasis in the Jordan Valley. "I put my hand in the trap," said Imad, still wondering how he found the courage to approach those bone-crushing jaws. "The hyena was trapped. I tried to calm him. I gave him water and stroked him. He didn't bite me and I finally got him out." Imad called a colleague at the Safari Zoo in Tel Aviv, and the zoo agreed to take the hyena. When the animal was healed, Imad released him in the same place he found him. "That is the only happy hyena story I have heard," I commented to Imad.

A single positive encounter between a man and a hyena, and a story of the courage to heal rather than destroy, is of course not enough to save a vulnerable species. And whether condemnations can change Palestinian public attitudes toward an animal surrounded by so many frightening stories is questionable. On the Facebook page "Palestine Wild", young men and women post photos they have taken of the flora and fauna of Palestine. Most photos are celebratory: the flowers of spring, an otter looking bemused, a male Palestine sunbird with his characteristic flash of blue. The only photo of a dead animal is—you've guessed it—a hyena tied to a car and looking, it must be said, quite grotesque to human eyes. However, the first comment, from a young woman, begins with a crucial question in capital letters: "WHY?" She goes on to ask why we humans kill anything that moves, and she salutes all those who try to preserve life and nature. Responses to her plea reflect the mixture of myth and confusion in young Palestinians' views of hyenas: one young man initially argues that hyenas are harmful—like wild boars—and could hurt children and thus should be killed. After another young man responds that hyenas in fact avoid humans, the first comes back and says perhaps hyenas should not be harmed. The young woman's "why?" seems to me like a good entry into a necessary public discussion.

"Why?" also brought me back to a place that might seem remote from hyena locales: Israel's military court near Ramallah, where young Palestinian men face trial, overwhelmingly on charges of "stone-throwing" at soldiers or settlers. I cannot discount other motives in the cruel and tragic encounter between young men and a hyena on a Hebron road, or indeed elsewhere where hyenas are killed (recall the drunk and thuggish young men from Beit Safafa). But I see young Palestinians coming to the defense of their unprotected communities using the only weapon they possess: the stones of our rocky landscape. Over the half century of military occupation, about one quarter of the Palestinian population, overwhelmingly but not exclusively male, has spent time in prison with charges ranging from the relatively rare armed activity to common offenses under prevailing military legislation of belonging to an illegal organization, possessing an illegal publication, or going to a demonstration. Today, defendants largely face the aforementioned simpler charge: stone-throwing.

Back in the 1980s, I had often found myself in a desolate and dirty hut just outside the Ramallah military court and prison complex, then in the heart of the town. I was a member of an informal faculty committee at Birzeit University assisting students and faculty detained by the Israeli army. We had little if any power to affect the proceedings, but, sitting on a scarred bench alongside family members, mostly mothers hoping to see their loved ones, we practiced the art of waiting. A particular master was philosopher Hugh Harcourt, who always had a paperback of the *Iliad* or Plato tucked in his knapsack.

After the 1993–1995 Oslo agreements, the military court moved several miles outside Ramallah to Ofer, as the military occupation relocated rather than dissolved. Several decades later, in the summer of 2016, I joined a visit to the Ofer military court organized by Military Court Watch, a local NGO. By a twist of fate, I was accompanying Nobel prize–winner Mario

Vargas Llosa, who was in Palestine to contribute to a book on the fiftieth anniversary of the occupation. I had just read his most recent book, *The Discreet Hero*, set in Lima, where the nickname for the two thuggish and parasitical sons of the main character was "the hyenas." While a hyena is a common figure for treachery and cowardice, it struck me as interesting that the hyena's reputation resonated in Peru. Peru is the home of many carnivores, including the jaguar and the spectacled bear, but not our less glamorous carrion eater, who has never set foot in South America. Clearly the millennia of hyena invective stretched across continents and lands, marking not only Vargas Llosa's unpleasant fictional characters but unconventional real-life rebels. When Mary Wollstonecraft published *A Vindication of the Rights of Woman* in 1792, writer and politician Horace Walpole promptly termed her a "hyena in petticoats."

On that hot June morning, we found ourselves witnessing the peculiarities of mammalian behavior in my corner of the world. We drove along a road from Jerusalem that was both familiar and strange: it used to lead to Ramallah, but access to my town has been blocked for sixteen years. Around the corner from Ofer is the Israeli settlement of Givat Zeev. With its villas and shopping centers, it has become a sizeable town. It inhabits land where a fertile wetland meadow once stood, which was seasonally flooded in winter and famous for its spring vegetables, as well as providing a welcoming home for birds, frogs, and other small creatures.

Entering the tin-walled waiting room at Ofer now, families sat on benches, hoping to be called to various makeshift courtrooms. I felt propelled back into the past: How could I have forgotten what it was like to wait for a brief glimpse of a son or a brother? Ramallah, with its cafés, art exhibits, and cultural festivals faded much farther away than the few miles that separated it from Ofer. I asked an especially pretty girl who she was waiting for. "My fiancé," she said shyly. "God willing, there will be good news," I said in my poor Arabic.

A thin, dignified father in a cheap nylon sports shirt wanted to talk. He was from Jalazoun refugee camp near Ramallah, and he had sons of sixteen and eighteen in prison. When the soldiers pounded on his door to detain his younger son, he rushed to the door to prevent it being blown up and told the soldiers "please be careful, there are small children here." Soldiers do not often listen to distraught fathers: one stepped on his sleeping six-year-old and another slapped his teenaged daughter when she tried to use her mobile phone to film the masked soldiers. Jalazoun camp is located near the Israeli settlement complex of Beit El; its proximity to settlers and the army that protects them makes it a continuous "friction point." "When the army's mission is to protect 500,000 settlers in the midst of a Palestinian population of 2.7 million," said attorney Gerard Horton from Military Court Watch, "the only way is mass intimidation." The father from Jalazoun refugee camp followed us out. He asked Mario, "Could you please tell me your name? My daughter at Birzeit University can google you and I can let my sons in prison know." Mario nodded gravely and supervised as I wrote the correct spelling on a torn piece of paper.

In one of the prefab courtrooms, we squeezed ourselves onto the sole bench provided for visitors. Soldiers ushered in three young Palestinian defendants. One youth raised his voice to tell his mother and sister that he was alright. Another stared at our crowded bench, hoping his mother would appear. We tried to look encouraging, but he bowed his head and rubbed his eyes. Each hearing lasted only a few minutes. A young female military judge presided, with each teenager represented by a weary Palestinian lawyer. All three defendants had confessed under interrogation, and all were charged with separate incidents of stone-throwing and sent back to prison. With the military court boasting a conviction rate of more than 99 percent, the main "work" of securing the confession falls to the brutalizing techniques employed by the arresting soldiers and interrogators before the court appearance.

In the courtroom that day, the young judge performed her military reserve duty in accordance with the military law in force. However, she functioned, as was so clear from the family members we spoke with, inside a matrix of control—of night raids and frightened families—that could only operate by fear. Fear is indeed the mythic hyena rather than the shy nocturnal creature that is subject to destruction. The young Jerusalem poet Najwan Darwish wrote:

> Once I tried to sit
> On one of the vacant seats of hope
> But the word "reserved"
> Squatted there like a hyena

There are few positive associations of hyenas, real or mythical, but in one recent instance, a hyena filled a very vacant seat of hope in an interesting turn of the human imagination. One scrawny hyena made a global impact in March 2016, when two scientists published a short piece in *The Zoology of the Middle East*, not a publication that often attracts world attention. The scientists reported the sighting more than a decade earlier of a striped hyena in the middle of a pack of seven gray wolves in Israel's Naqab (Negev) Desert, apparently hunting together, noting an additional finding, also in the 1990s, of tracks of a hyena and three wolves. While the scientists cautiously opined that this could be an unusual symbiosis—cooperation between carnivores—or a "singular aberration," journalists seized on the story, casting the hyena and wolves as harbingers of peace. The *Washington Post's* headline was the clincher: "Wolves and hyenas hunt together, prove Middle East peace is possible." The *Post* continued: "There's been a Middle East peace pact for some time now. The deal was struck quietly in the arid desert of Israel probably because the two sides decided they needed each other to survive."

A lone sighting of a hyena in the midst of wolves, cooperating in a scrabble for survival: we humans in what Mark Twain aptly termed a "heart-broken land" cling to a new animal metaphor. Meanwhile, a Wall separates both hyenas and humans, and a politics of fear is unlikely to be shaken by a fragile hope witnessed in the desert. For me, Abu Hassan, maimed but alive in his cage within an imprisoned city, evokes more powerful associations. I think of the boys and young men captive in Ofer, sometimes for confronting soldiers with the ubiquitous stones in our limestone landscape, sometimes, like Abu Hassan, for being in the wrong place at the wrong time. Neither the boys nor the hyena are metaphors for each other, and young Palestinians have little sympathy and much aversion for Abu Hassan. Nonetheless, both in many ways are the hunted. Common lives in Palestine come in strange shapes.

Tribe of goats enjoying spring greenery near Palestinian village of Kfar Nimeh. *(Credit: Emile Ashrawi)*

CHAPTER 3

FLOCKS BY DAY: GOATS, SHEEP, AND SHEPHERDS UNDER THREAT

The southern Hebron Hills have a hint of green in the January weather. As a longtime resident of occupied Palestine, I have lived through many decidedly unholy moments and am usually immune to the "Biblical feel" of the Palestinian landscape that strikes many visitors. However, I succumb for a moment to the temptation to view shepherds and their flocks on these ancient hills as emblematic of an enduring tradition in Palestine. Then I shake myself out of my reverie; Amro, a livestock expert from the United Nations Food and Agricultural Organization, and I are about to visit a small herding community where that tradition is very much under threat.

South of the Palestinian city of Hebron close to the Green Line, the 1949 Armistice Line that became the 1967 "border" separating the West Bank from Israel, we turn off the main road. A bumpy dirt track takes us up to Khirbet Zanuta, where shepherds and their flocks live a precarious life. *Khirba* in Arabic indicates that, at one time in the past, the place was a ruin. It is a fairly common prefix to hilltop sites in historic Palestine, where civilization after civilization, community after community, settled and left behind their mark. Sheep and goats have been a constant presence in this landscape through all these human transformations. A 1917 handbook written for British troops in Palestine evoked this pastoral vision: "Flocks of sheep and goats, led out of a morning and back of an evening from every village and Bedouin encampment scour the country for pasturage all the year through."

But a troubled century has passed since then, and the four sunburned men, all shepherds, who greet us with ready handshakes and shy smiles have very contemporary problems. In Khirbet Zanuta, home to twenty-seven families and one hundred and thirty people, *Khirba* not only indicates a past ruin but the threat of becoming a ruin once again. The men usher us to plastic chairs, and we sit outside in the clear winter sunshine; paper cups of strong coffee are produced for the guests. A woman in the distance shoos chickens and geese, and I wonder if she made our delicious cardamom-scented coffee. Cooking and cleaning in Zanuta must be difficult: the only water source is a restored Roman cistern and occasional tank deliveries. Zanuta is not connected to either a water network or an electricity grid, so much depends on the functioning of two generators. Families live in makeshift stone structures supplemented by plastic covering, tin, and old tires. Whether these are upgrades from the caves that Zanuta residents inhabited until dampness finally rendered them unstable in the 1980s is doubtful. A slew of Israeli military edicts forbid Zanuta residents from erecting permanent dwellings, and even these improvised huts are under constant threat of demolition. Zanuta and its surrounding land have the misfortune to be in Area C, where the only authority is Israel, its army, and its poorly named Civil Administration.

Fayez, a stocky man with a broad face, works as a part-time nurse in a Hebron hospital; herding does not always suffice to support a family, especially in hemmed-in Zanuta. He points to the Separation Wall to the south of Zanuta, partly built on the village's land. To the east, on the hills and spring where Zanuta flocks used to graze and drink, is the Israeli settlement and industrial zone of Shima, a line of solar panels gleaming in the sunlight. Tene, another settlement, can be seen from the west. Even much of the land outside the settlement boundaries is off-limits for Zanuta's flocks. With such severe restrictions, Zanuta shepherds must now pay for feed for their animals as well as for water delivered by trucker tanks. Amro and his organization have been responsible for supplying Zanuta herders with seeds of barley and vetch, a plant in the pea family often grown for fodder, to plant on the small patch of remaining land.

On the other side of the Wall, on the southern slopes of the Hebron Hills, we see the tempting but unreachable forest of Yattir, the largest planted forest in Israel. Its eponymous settlement is on the West Bank side of the Green Line but outside the Wall, whose path often carves itself inside occupied territory. The Wall itself is illegal under international law, according to the 2004 ruling of the International Court of Justice at the Hague. But the ruling, unenforced and unobserved, does not help those affected by either the course of the Wall or relentless Israeli settlement expansion. For Zanuta shepherds and farmers, there is only persistence: "Every spring I plant in the valley even though they have taken the mountain," says Fayez.

Amro has explained to me that Zanuta herders are "villagers with the herding ways of Bedouins," meaning that they shepherd mixed flocks of goats and sheep, and unlike many villagers, keep their flocks outside their living area rather than in a stable under the house. Amro surprises me by temporarily changing the subject away from his passionate interest in livestock, asking if any of the men have more than one wife, and everyone laughs. "One is enough," says an older man. The men admit that wives have most of the hard jobs, making yoghurt, buttermilk, and cheese from the flock's milk, while men have the easier job of selling the same. When one accounts for time spent chasing chickens and hissing geese, or trying to keep children and dwellings clean and healthy in Zanuta's difficult circumstances, women's work must be endless. As a result, says a young man shyly, girls don't always want to marry them. "My wife is younger than her sister," Taysir tells me with a wry grin. "But her sister married an employee: she looks ten years younger than my wife." "Employee"—whether with UNRWA, the Palestinian Authority, or private business—is a sacred category in Palestine, denoting stability and a regular wage.

Abu Hani, whose three daughters are in primary school, adds another problem: the only school is in the town of Dhahiriya, fifteen miles away. The family tried to stay together in Zanuta, but the sole erratic bus left Dhahiriya too early for the girls to return home. They now live largely with their grandmother in Dhahiriya and Abu Hani's wife often stays in the town. "And why do you stay?" I ask. "I didn't get an education myself," he replies softly. "We can't keep our flocks in town: we can't raise a herd on a dunum of land. The land is our inheritance." Taysir adds comfortingly that the children always come in the spring.

The inheritance is, however, under threat. The flocks of goats and sheep of Zanuta not only cannot reach much of their old grazing ground but their numbers have been depleted by climatic processes as well. In 2007, a Palestinian survey estimated Zanuta livestock at four thousand sheep and eight hundred goats. But loss of grazing land and threats to the village's very existence escalated that year because of another menace: drought. I had not really grasped the significance of the regional drought that began in 2006 and went on for almost five years. To be sure, drought years are a persistent feature of life in the Middle East: in 1933, a severe drought year, British Mandate officials reported that villagers and nomads in the northern Safad region of Palestine lost 75 percent of their livestock. But today, with global warming, cycles of drought have become more sustained and their effects longer lasting.

Amro patiently explained the consequences of the 2006–2011 drought in Palestine. As pasturage withered and feed prices soared, herders were forced to sell some of their animals: overall there was a reduction of flocks by about one-third. When I visited Dr. Iyad Adra, the chief veterinarian at Palestine's Ministry of Agriculture in Ramallah, he added that the drought also propelled lifestyle changes as herding and farming families tried to diversify by urging "one child to become an employee, another to work in Israel."

We town-dwellers ignore both the existence and consequences of longer-term drought at our peril as climate change, or catastrophic climate breakdown, to borrow environmentalist writer George Monbiot's term, takes its toll. Our historical imagination places Palestine firmly in the aptly named Fertile Crescent, comprising also modern-day Lebanon, Syria, and Iraq, whose alluvial plains allowed the birth of agriculture, cities, and civilizations. But increasingly, the countries of the Fertile Crescent are described as "arid lands." This is perhaps not breaking news: nineteenth-century European and American travelers issued a constant stream of complaint about Palestine's lack of green fields and forests. In his account of an 1867 visit, Mark Twain decried a desolate landscape: "There was hardly a tree or a shrub anywhere. Even the olive and the cactus, those fast friends of a worthless soil, had almost deserted." Twain, however, traveled to Palestine in the "hot season." The summer dry season is part of Mediterranean life, and locals, unlike Twain and his band, try to stay out of the midday sun. One feels Twain's relief whenever he encounters a grove of lemon trees, a spring, or the still-green areas near the town of Nablus.

A telling contrast to Twain's response to the Palestinian landscape can be found in the recently published diaries of the poet Siegfried Sassoon, who, after his stint in an Edinburgh hospital where he was treated for shell shock from his time in the trenches of World War I, was sent briefly to Palestine in the spring of 1918. Nina Martyris, writing in the *Los Angeles Review of Books*, has provided us with excerpts from his diary during his stay in Palestine. The poet, heartbroken by war, finds relief wandering over the Ramallah hills as the land's "shy and lovely austerity" reveals itself to him. He listens to the gurgle of streams, the sound of birds (he counts fifty species), and sights a gazelle trotting quietly away. On one serene ramble outside Ramallah he writes: "I escaped from the war completely for four hours." Palestine, he affirmed, was his Arcadia.

It is heartening to remember Sassoon's vision as we contemplate the problems of both the present and the past. When long-term drought is combined with the seemingly endless wars of our times, the mix is toxic to animals and humans alike. A century ago, the horrors of World War I in Palestine and the region were compounded by drought and the related and highly devastating 1915 locust invasion, whose swarms appeared near Jerusalem "in such density that they eclipsed the sun," according to the memoirs of Jerusalemite Sami Hadawi. Two photographs from that time show the Garden of Gethsemane in bloom one day and the next stripped of all vegetation. Today, the deadly brew of human conflict and natural disaster spreads another blight not only in Palestine but across the region.

Across the border in Syria in the last decade, drought—and its mismanagement by the central government—has had dramatic consequences. Syria's fertile Haroun plain has long been one of the region's main breadbaskets. But for five years, beginning in 2006, up to 60 percent of Syria's land experienced, as one expert put it, perhaps too dramatically, "the worst long-term drought and most severe set of crop failures since agricultural civilizations began in the Fertile Crescent many millennia ago." Herders in the northeast lost around 85 percent of their livestock, affecting more than a million people. The consequences of drought and government incapacities included loss of livelihoods, extreme poverty, and food insecurity, all drivers of the 2011 rebellion that erupted in Syria. That civilian uprising against a dictatorial regime, thanks to the external actors and militarization that plague our region, morphed into a bloody and tragic conflict that to date has killed more than a quarter of a million people and propelled endless streams of refugees. The toll on animals remains uncounted.

Throughout the older cycles of drought in Palestine and the region, goats have persisted while other animals faltered. Goats can survive in scrubland and continue to produce milk even when the land's deeply rooted weeds, twigs, and dry grasses are the only food available. Goats (*Capra hircus*) are one of the earlier domesticated animals: bones of a domesticated goat found in Jericho were dated to around 7000 BCE. Joy Hinson, in her book *Goat*, gives us one illustration of the significance of goats in Palestine and the Eastern Mediterranean, noting that there are ten different words for goats in the Bible, seven in Hebrew and three in Greek. No one seems to have counted the words for sheep, but one suspects they may be equally numerous. Sheep were domesticated even earlier than goats—probably in Iran—and belong to the same subfamily, Caprinae, as goats.

Both sheep and goats are cloven-hoofed ruminants with four-chambered stomachs. The fourth is similar to our stomach; the other chambers ferment and regurgitate and ferment again the cellulite-rich diet until it can be digested in number four. Despite their omnivorous reputation, goats are in fact rather selective eaters, using their tongue and lips to check out the fare. They are more physically flexible than their sheep cousins, who graze on grass, while goats often prefer nutritious weeds and are also browsers, standing on their hind legs to access leaves and other delicacies out of reach of sheep.

The goat's admirable survival skills make it well adapted to Palestine's stony landscape and seasonal shifts from a verdant landscape in the winter rainy season to parched yellow fields and valleys in summer. One hot June morning, I drove along the road Palestinians call Wadi Nar, the Valley of Fire. Wadi Nar winds its way through the arid landscape below Jerusalem and is the only road between the northern and southern West Bank available to Palestinians who have no permits to enter Jerusalem. On one side of the road the forbidden city of Jerusalem rose up; on the other, two small herds of black goats were grazing on stony hills where I could not discern even a trace of green, let alone a patch of shade. Admirable, indeed.

So why, we might enquire, did a British Mandatory official in the 1940s declare the goat Public Enemy Number One? This is particularly odd given the sustained human conflict between Zionist Jews and Palestinian Arabs during the Mandate period. Surely, there was plenty of human enmity to address without targeting goats. Nonetheless, our weed-eating ruminant definitely got the goat of British official E. H. Taylor of the Soil Conservation Board. Taylor was the author of a 1940s pamphlet titled *Save Our Soil*, which announced the goat as the culprit behind the scourge of overgrazing. The pamphlet was translated into

Arabic and displayed a tantalizing photo of green rolling hills captioned "Typical English Countryside." This imperial vision of re-creating green England in unwelcoming climates was one the British pursued in other colonial ventures, but underlying it were often more mundane economic interests. In India, the British Empire's Indian Forest Act of 1878, called by Indian scholars Guha and Gadgil a "model for other colonies," gave an environmental justification for its dispossession of Indian peasants but crucially was motivated by the need for wood to build the Indian railway network and the ships of the British navy and merchant fleets. Reviewing the achievements of forestry in Palestine in a 1948 article in the aptly named *Empire Forestry Review*, two British officials cited the "distinct contribution" of Palestine's forests during World War II.

The creation of a separate Department of Forestry in Palestine and its relatively ambitious afforestation plans—including vigorous anti-goat campaigns—came only in 1936 as the Great Arab Revolt against British rule erupted and a number of the wooded areas of the central hills became Palestinian rebel strongholds and thus off-limits for British tree-planting. But even while chasing rebels, British officials maintained their enmity toward goats, with strong aversion as well to sheep and camels, citing the plight of the hapless tree-planter as "an unwilling but helpless supplier of free fodder." The native black goat in Palestine, sometimes called the Nubian goat, was deemed to have particularly bad habits, and plans were devised to replace her with the Damascus goat, also named the Shami goat, Sham being another name for Damascus. (The British also called her the Cyprus goat, as she came to Palestine via Cyprus.) The Shami goat's attractive portrait and her high milk yield statistics were widely circulated to peasants and settlers alike. Other British schemes advocated replacing goats altogether with sheep, or, in a grander vision, substituting cows and presumably the greener fields needed to sustain them. This plan made little ecological sense but nonetheless was attractive to the new Jewish immigrants from Europe.

Palestine had (and has) real environmental problems that cannot all be blamed, however tempting it is to do so, on British colonial machinations. Along with the devastating deforestation of Palestine in World War I came soil erosion, particularly when terracing was not practiced and winter rains washed soil unimpeded down from the central highlands. And admittedly, grazing, whether over- or not, was a shaper of the landscape. Nonetheless, it is hard to see goats, rather than human armies, as the prime cause of Palestine's ecological woes, or an increase in cows as an environmental benefit. Indeed, we know in hindsight what damage, including a major contribution to global warming through the release of methane gas by their digestive habits, has been triggered worldwide by the exponential growth in the raising of cows for meat and milk. And new Australian studies suggest that grazing, particularly of sheep, has some benefits for biodiversity, as these ruminants pass seeds and moisture to arid land.

Throughout the Mandate, beleaguered British officials kept trying to produce quick fixes through draconian legislation. One of the most drastic was a 1946 edict, admittedly a failure, which ordered licensing of all shepherds and the wearing of metal identification tags; restrictions were also placed on the number of total livestock in each "control area." A prize for the most unrealistic goal should have been given to Gilbert Sale, Palestine's first conservator of forests. As the British Mandate drew to a close, Sale proposed a scheme to reduce the number of goats to one hundred thousand. When the British withdrew from Palestine in December 1947, however, there were, by conservative estimate, three-quarters of a million goats in Palestine and about a quarter million sheep. In this round, goats clearly defeated the prevailing authority.

The new state of Israel was, however, more successful. A main reason was offered without further comment by the new chief forester, A. Y. Goor, who wrote that "the problem of over-grazing has become less acute since the Arabs left the country taking most of their flocks with them," surely one of the most understated evocations of the Palestinian nakba (catastrophe). Goor estimated that only 150,000 goats were left out of perhaps 650,000, but that number, it seems, was still far too many. Israel enacted the 1950 Plant Protection Act, also known as the Goat Damage Law, which banned black goats—and their Bedouin and peasant owners—from much of their old grazing ground, some of it newly forested in Israel's massive planting of European pines. Called "pine deserts" by environmentalists, these new woodlands were often situated near or on the ruins of Palestinian villages. The black goat population shrunk to about two thousand in the Mount Carmel region of the Galilee. More than sixty-five years later, in December 2017, Ayman Odeh, a Palestinian member of the Knesset, Israel's legislature, introduced a bill to repeal the law, which has passed a preliminary reading. The realization had finally dawned that goats could help prevent the endemic forest fires that often swept the country, by grazing on the flammable shrubs, pine seeds, and undergrowth that ignite these fires.

Today, in the slice of historic Palestine that is governed by the Palestinian Authority (or inhabited by Palestinians in Area C), the Palestinian Bureau of Statistics counts about 750,000 sheep and 250,000 goats, with the Hebron district having the largest proportion. There are only 34,000 cows, with the northern West Bank around the town of Jenin having the majority. Inside Israel, the proportions are different, with about 480,000 sheep, 125,000 dairy cows, and about 100,000 goats. Israel's count includes the black Nubian goats in the herds of the remaining Bedouin communities of the Naqab (Neger) Desert, the remaining black goats in the Galilee, and Shami goats residing in the boutique goat farms in the Jerusalem area and Galilee which produce expensive cheeses for the Israeli market, as well as mixed flocks.

Even in the last four or five years without drought, Zanuta herders cannot count on the winter rains for pasture to graze their flocks. In better times Bedouins and other herders in the West Bank used to rely on seven to eight months of grazing. In the remaining summer months, the shepherds had to find feed for their animals. Now the proportion is reversed, due primarily to Israeli restrictions on access to grazing land and water and compounded by cycles of drought. Yet, during our visit the Zanuta flocks were still out on a neighboring barren hill because, as Taysir tells us, goats and sheep need exercise. Amro is not convinced; he thinks that the roaming flock will lose weight and thus value. "But shepherds are stone-minded," he tells me in a loud whisper. I nonetheless side with the shepherds and their flock on the pleasures of a daily excursion.

Taysir brings us a round of sweetened drinks and biscuits. The list of problems and deprivations continues and is bitter: along with no schools and no connections to electricity or water networks, there is no clinic in the village and no doctor, apart from Saturday visits from the voluntary Medical Relief Committee, a longstanding Palestinian NGO. "We will die before getting to the hospital," Fayez says. It is no wonder that Taysir, leaning on his stick, invokes the Prophet Muhammad before answering my question about the main problems facing Zanuta: "The Wall. Settlements. Everything."

And everything includes, I learn, a decade-long court battle against the Israeli authorities' order to "uproot," in Faisal's words, the whole community. The first demolition order from the Israel Defense Forces' Civil Administration came in 2007; the grounds of the eviction, familiar to many Palestinian communities in Area C, were that Zanuta's structures had no building permits. This is of course true: Israel does not give building permits to Palestinians in Area C. The Association of Civil Rights in Israel (ACRI) came to Zanuta's defense and has continued to counter a range of State arguments in a seemingly endless stream of court hearings: that Zanuta residents were new to the site (ACRI produced pre-1967 aerial photographs), that there is no zoning plan (ACRI countered that Israel has not permitted such plans in Area C and asked that one be drawn up), and that Zanuta must be demolished to protect archeological ruins. Israeli archeologist Dr. Avi Ofer, who has worked on the site, gave an affidavit to the court describing how Zanuta residents could in fact help preserve the remnants of historic buildings in the area. Continuously inhabited at least since Byzantine times, Zanuta does indeed bear the traces of the past, as do innumerable other sites in Palestine. Emek Shaveh, an organization of progressive Israeli archeologists, states it saliently: "Every Palestinian village has ruins."

Court orders were accompanied by military action. In 2012, soldiers demolished two cisterns and tore down several sheep pens. But as the shadows lengthened around us on that January day, Fayez and the others were most worried about the upcoming hearing in the Israeli High Court, which they could not attend themselves, having no permits to enter Jerusalem. When I later called the ACRI to find out what had happened in the Zanuta hearing, Yoran Kilner, its spokesperson, was at first unsure. It is clearly hard to remember the serial hearings of a small community amid all the other violations that ACRI is contesting, including the fate of twelve neighboring herding villages who have the temerity to live in an area the Israeli army has designated as Firing Zone 918; the case on their eviction has been going on now for fifteen years. When Yoran got back to me on Zanuta's case, it was with news of yet another court hearing in the offing. At the January session, the State "had announced it is reexamining criteria for building approval in Area C" but in the meantime wanted to go ahead with demolishing buildings in Zanuta that it claimed were damaging the archeological site. ACRI objected and Yoran added that the Association believes that the State will never allow the drawing up of a plan for the village. In another hearing in September 2017, the court "decided to delete" ACRI's petition while the Israeli military "deliberates" introducing changes to its planning criteria in Area C.

What are the effects on Zanuta families when year after year they face the delivery of demolition orders, court postponements, and threatening visits by soldiers? After a trip to Palestine with the Palestine Festival of Literature, Teju Cole wrote an essay entitled "Bad Laws" that captured for me what happens to Palestinians who are victims not only of military might but what Cole terms "cold violence," in a toxic mix with other forms of intimidation. A "dizzying assemblage of laws and bylaws, contracts, ancient documents, force, amendments, customs, religion, conventions and sudden irrational moves," Cole writes, pushes "people into deep uncertainty about the fundamentals of life, over years and decades." Living with such profound insecurity exhausts the soul. Waiting for a 2013 court hearing, a Palestinian woman in yet another threatened village in the southern Hebron Hills succinctly told a *Haaretz* journalist how such cold violence affected her: "All the time we are tired from our thoughts," Mugaiza said. "What if they throw us out of our home?"

Tales of cold violence do not have the immediate narrative power of a dramatic incident of hot violence. If each story is told just for its bare facts, each story sounds the same: demolition orders, land confiscation, settler violence, the killing or confiscation of Palestinian livestock, the list goes on and on. Even the staunch *Haaretz* journalist Amira Hass wonders who listens. Just before our trip to Zanuta, Hass gave yet another meticulous account of cold violence: Israel, by military order, demolished 151 Palestinian structures in the first week of 2017, including sixty-five in Area C and seven rain cisterns. This is four times the average month's demolition in 2016. She continued her reporting throughout the year with a slew of smaller stories, some of cold violence, some hot. In April 2017, Israeli settlers killed a sheep and wounded two goats belonging to a family in the northern Jordan Valley. While this incident passed without great notice, pictures of slaughtered sheep captured a rare headline in late February 2018, when masked settlers from an "illegal outpost" (illegal also under Israeli law) killed ten sheep belonging to a farmer from the village of Einabus. In the same week, settlers from another illegal outpost in the Jordan Valley used a more sophisticated method to terrorize sheep, sending drones over a flock from the village of Al-Aqabah. And so it goes, to echo Kurt Vonnegut. When lives become statistics and stories are suffused with repetition, our attention wavers. The Haifa-based Palestinian writer Ala Hlehel was chillingly honest when he accompanied a number of international writers to another threatened khirba in the Hebron Hills—Khirbet Umm Al-Khair—where homes had been demolished by Israeli bulldozers just a few days before. An agitated old man whose house had just been destroyed jumped from one writer to the next, trying to tell his story, and Ala took him aside to film him. After twenty minutes Ala admitted: "My arm is getting tired, my eye is getting tired . . . then I realize I am a little bored. This discovery kills me." Like Mugaiza facing the demolition of her home or Ala hearing an old man's story over and over again, we are tired from our thoughts. To stay hopeful, one must take time to just sit in the sun, on a green January day, enjoying the banter of the four shepherds who laugh even more than they complain, and gaze at the lovely way the southern hills roll down to the Jordan Valley.

In Zanuta, the sun is high and it is time to leave. Just as I ask, "Where are the sheep?" an older man herds a flock of fifty or so into a nearby pen. I think at first that they are all goats, several of whom perch on top of the pen rather than inside it. On our drive to Hebron, Amro has given me an emergency briefing on the two kinds of goats: the native Palestinian or Nubian black goat, the target of British officials during the Mandate and Israel after 1948, and the more prized Shami goat. Indeed, the Shami goat was recently extolled on the GoatWorld website (check it out) by two Israeli goat breeders as possessing "a particularly aristocratic bearing, great nobility and charisma," as well as expressive eyes and long ears. Their view is shared by many in a region where Israeli and Arab perspectives are usually diverse. Amro showed me a picture on his phone of a Shami goat in Saudi Arabia that was featured at the annual goat beauty contest in Riyadh and valued at about 450,000 Saudi riyals, or $120,000. An elegant goat, indeed.

Goat beauty contests are not unknown in Palestine, and in more cooperative times seem to have starred goats on both sides of the Green Line. Shami goats are still prized by owners for their appearance. Recently, Amro was called upon for a Shami goat emergency in the Palestinian village of Silwan, near

Jerusalem. He administered medicine for a lung infection to a Shami goat that was kept in the family's salon during the cold winter for warmth. These goats are more susceptible to both heat and cold than our run-of the-mill Nubian goat; they need more food and water but produce more milk. And truly they are beautiful: stroking the head of a pregnant white Shami goat one sultry afternoon in Beit Sahur, I was delighted to meet such a lovely creature. I recall Picasso's pet goat, Esmeralda, who was not as attractive, at least from the artist's sculptures of her, but was much beloved. Picasso let her sleep in an upstairs bedroom near him because, he said, she might get lonely during the night.

I look at the herd again, trying to make out who is a sheep and who is a goat. Alas, Amro neglected to brief me on the two breeds of sheep, one of which, the native Awassi, has a goat-like appearance from the head up, with males sporting elegant curved horns. The separation of the sheep and the goats, in the New Testament account, is a moral mission (those who are like sheep are sorted onto the blessed side of Christ's throne), but I find the task of classification more daunting. Israeli breeders produced the second, also popular, sheep, the hornless Assaf, by crossbreeding the Awassi with the European East Freisan sheep. Like the Shami goat, the Assaf is at least half a native. The categories of native and indigenous are never set in stone, whether for goats or humans. And fortunately, the Assaf inherited an important characteristic from the Awassi: a fat tail, sometimes called a flat tail, where nutrients can be stored for the lean times in our dry climate. However, Assaf sheep, now the majority in Palestine because their milk yield is higher, are less resistant to disease. In the midst of these tangled genealogies, I am drawn to the simpler language of shepherds: goats are *samra* (black) and sheep are *bayda* (white), whatever their actual color.

An unmistakable goat teeters on the swaying gate of the pen but does not lose its balance. Goats are great escape artists; I wonder why this fine creature doesn't take the leap to freedom. Perhaps it has a fondness for company, as goats are social animals, or perhaps it is simply waiting to be fed. I fall into anthropomorphic speculation: Is it curious about us? Does he wonder what I am doing on this January afternoon, hanging around its pen? A more reasonable question is whether goats are insatiably curious or are just continually looking for something to eat as they climb the most unlikely verticals.

In a story he set sometime in the last years of the nineteenth century, Yitzhak (or Ishaq) Shami, born and raised in the Sephardic Jewish community in Hebron, opted for curiosity. (Shami himself is not named after a goat but from real or putative family origins in Syria). An Arab Jew, he wrote in Hebrew, but his terrain was the society and people around him, both Arab and Jew. Describing the launching of a horse race between two camps of Palestinian Arabs about to set out for the traditional Muslim procession to Nebi Musa, the shrine of Moses, Shami wrote: "The goats in both camps, not easily subdued by commands, broke through the lines of horsemen, ran madly about, some even climbing up onto camels and other high places to get a better look at the proceedings."

I test my opinion of goat intelligence on Amro, who simply shakes his head: "Goats are stupid." Sheep have even worse reputations, although recent research has highlighted their social and emotional intelligence, noting that sheep can recognize each other's faces (up to fifty!), something humans might find challenging when faced with a uniformly fluffy flock. The matriarch of the herd is also cited for her leadership abilities. Goats cannot be far behind: in one of the most eccentric explorations of what it is like to be a goat (and to take a "holiday from being human"), Thomas Thwaites donned a prosthetic contraption to allow him to walk like a goat, over the Alps no less, and learned what it is to think with his mouth, rather than his eyes. The brain is embodied, he wisely notes. And Shami was right; goats are what is called in the language of animal behavior "neophilic." Faced with a new experience, a goat is curious and moves to explore it, rather than retreating to the flock and hunkering down like a sheep. On his stroll in the Alps, Thwaites grazed on grass that he then spat out in his "rumen bag" and later, desperate for nourishment, cooked in a pressure cooker. After testing it with chemicals he dug in and ate "the most unappetizing meal of my life: burnt grass stew." His appreciation for the four-chambered stomach, as well as goatish intelligence and nimbleness, grew apace.

We examine a pregnant goat who has lost patches of her hair: Amro says she needs medicine, but the old man says her hair will grow back once she has a kid. Amro makes a last-ditch effort to convince the shepherds to add more protein and vitamins to the feed. "Can you live on bread alone?" he asks rhetorically. You need modern medicine, Amro advises the bemused shepherds, not just your traditional herbal remedies like fenugreek and wild thyme. Fayez and the others refrain from pointing out that neither human doctors nor the vets from the Ministry of Agriculture are regular visitors to Zanuta.

I wonder when I will be able to return to Zanuta, and whether there will still be shepherds and flocks to greet me. Zanuta's flock of goats and sheep have one advantage over their human counterparts who are plagued with deep uncertainty about the future. The flock lives in the present tense. Stuck with human worries about the future, I decide to explore herding and farming communities further: surely, somewhere there is a bit of stability for humans and a pasture, even with a few stones and thorns, for a herd.

It is springtime in Palestine, and as the flowering landscape rolls by our United Nations SUV, I am pleased just to be out of my Ramallah enclave, heading out to visit a farming community and several Bedouin encampments in the northern West Bank. My companion, Intissaar, is a sturdy, pleasant young woman from a Nablus village. A graduate in agricultural engineering from Najah University, she, like Amro, is currently working for the United Nations Food and Agriculture Organization (FAO). I try to enjoy the journey and forget the tension of Palestine road travel. But turning west off the main road to Nablus, I automatically snarl at the entrance to Yitzhar settlement, home to some of the most extreme and violent Israeli settlers. A 2015 petition to the Israeli High Court by Israeli human rights organizations asked the State to take action against the chief rabbi of Yitzhar, Yosef Elitzar, for his writings calling for violence against Arabs, finally leading to his indictment in June 2017; the case has not yet been heard. I relax as the road curves north; we are still in the central highlands, but the valley widens and the views toward the coast are lovely. We drive through Silet ed-Daher, a village famous for meat; a black-and-white cow stands outside a roadside butcher awaiting his fate.

Our destination is the hilltop village of Al-Mughayyir, where poor households keep small flocks of sheep and are recipients of the same FAO seed program that was at work in Zanuta. We are on what the United Nations calls an evaluation mission, which inevitably means filling out long forms. I have found myself in the familiar Palestinian world of donors and beneficiaries. Intissaar is charged by her organization with locating and interviewing at least six recipients. The ride to Al-Mughayyir from the town of Jenin is beautiful; the hills are forested and the fields a bright green. Suddenly, a hotel and Ferris wheel eerily appear in the midst of a large field. This is the Haddad Resort, which opened, rather bravely, in 2005 after four years of the Second Palestinian Intifada. Alongside uncertainty, or as a response to it, Palestinians have a passion for normalcy: to give their kids a ride on a Ferris wheel and to sip fruit juice by a pool in a green field.

As we drive through Al-Mughayyir, the houses become more run-down; when we arrive at our destination, we find two small concrete buildings edged around a *hoash*, or court-yard. One building is whitewashed, a family dwelling, and one with dark curtains holds bleating sheep. It is a version of the old peasant house where animals were kept on the ground floor, close at hand and safe from predators. In the court-yard, two women are baking bread on a cast-iron dome over a wood fire, a method that produces one of the world's more delicious breads. The most active cook, Raqiyya, is the official seed recipient, as she is the owner and tender of the sheep that are sweltering in the darkened shed behind a hot oven. A tall, middle-aged woman with a strong face and physique, she is clearly in charge of more than the baking of bread.

In many villages like Al-Mughayyir in the first quarter century of the occupation, Palestinian men often worked inside Israel as laborers, most often in construction, while women kept the house—and the fields and livestock—going. Men returned only on the weekend. Labor markets were thus highly gendered and women's formal labor participation quite low, despite rising levels of education. Today, men have difficulties obtaining permits to enter Israel to work, but women still take on quite a bit of agricultural work, which is usually family work and unpaid.

Raqiyya, however, is at the head of the family's livestock enterprise and thus, to her annoyance, the target of a barrage of questions as Intissaar valiantly attempts to fill out the questionnaire she has on a small iPad. How many family members? Eight. Do you have any employees? Raqiyya looks puzzled and snaps a few twigs for the fire before shaking her head in a decisive *no*. A handsome rooster enters the courtyard. Several men also arrive and we all sit on plastic chairs except busy Raqiyya and her companion, a gaunt woman who squats by the sheep hut and occasionally provides a piece of firewood.

"What is your monthly income?" Intisaar asks. Raqiyya is stumped but valiantly makes a guess, adding that family income isn't steady and "every month is different." Alas, a problematic entry for United Nations statistics; fluctuations in income are more the rule than the exception for rural families. Raqiyya is, however, very clear answering whether everyone who got seeds used them. "We are all *fellah* (peasants) so of course we used them." But then she completely loses patience when Intissaar asks the last two crucial queries for donor reporting: Who is the executing agency? Who is the donor? A seed recipient from another family, Walid, who is sitting nearby, knows the name of the agency—the Food and Agriculture Organization of the United Nations (FAO), of course—but doesn't know who the donor is. "Canada," Intisaar says succinctly, and there is a general sigh of relief at learning the correct answer. Two more seed recipients arrive and, with an air of resignation, strive to answer the questions. A chubby man, Ibrahim, who has been sitting quietly throughout our encounter, goes into gear. When both recipients are bewildered at the donor question, Ibrahim looks innocently to the heavens and whispers softly but audibly "Canada." "He is cheating," says Intissaar, doing her best to look stern.

The Al-Mughayyir farmers have small flocks of about twenty to thirty sheep, with no goats in sight. Only Hassan, who is also employed as a policeman, has a larger flock of fifty sheep. One old woman we visit, sitting outside another small concrete hut with her walker beside her, has only seventeen sheep, all crowded into the hut behind her. Despite the green fields we traveled through, sheep in Al-Mughayyir have only one chance a year to graze—after the wheat is harvested, when they are finally let into the fields. The barley and vetch grown from the seeds are thus crucial to their survival. On the edge of the village, a woman who is requesting a cistern to provide water for her animals points to the Wall, only about a half mile away. "There was a spring there," she explains. This sylvan landscape is also a geography of loss. Hospitality, however, is at the ready. We have to refuse the increasingly insistent and kind invitations to lunch, having already consumed three coffees, two teas, and a sugary fruit juice drink; Intissaar and I are beginning to whisper bathroom jokes to each other. But we must go on, down the slopes of the Jordan Valley to visit several Bedouin families.

"That's the worst checkpoint in the world," said Intissaar, a bold claim in Palestine, the land of more than four hundred checkpoints and obstacles. We are driving south from the town of Toubas, deeper and lower into the northern Jordan Valley. The checkpoint, unmanned today, separates Toubas, in Area A under the Palestinian Authority, from the vast stretches of the valley in Area C. At first the land is not so steep and desolate. The wadis are dusted with a fine coat of early spring green, a green that spreads in late winter to the hills of the Jerusalem wilderness and Jordan Valley and will be gone by summer until another year. Driving to Jericho from Jerusalem in the early spring, I often have thought that the buried seeds provoked by rain into green sprouts each year are the best example I know of Nietzche's notion of eternal recurrence. But the Jordan Valley today contains less hopeful messages.

This should be the time and place when shepherds lead their flocks to this recurring brief green gauze over the land in order to graze on these miraculous verdant shoots emerging from stone. But there are no herders, no sheep, no goats, no one. Instead there are signs posted with a terrible regularity: WARNING: MILITARY AREA. Almost half—45 percent—of the hills and wadis of the Jordan Valley are at present such closed military zones. A staggering 85 percent of the Valley is designated as Area C. It is only when we get to more rugged terrain where a dry wadi cuts into a steep slope of rock and thistles that we find two Bedouin black tents and a row of plastic sheds perched above the wadi. A barefoot boy with flashing eyes dashes up the slope to greet us and invite us down to the tents. We are in Wadi al Malha (sometimes called al-Malih), named for a nearby spring that must, according to its name, host some form of salt deposits. The land is stony with streaks of black; a geologist colleague later tells me that Wadi al Malha is rich with mineral resources, such as clay for making cement, although none of these can be extracted by Palestinians. Further down, as the wadi nears the border, there are three Israeli nature reserves marked only by small signs from the Israel Nature and Parks Authority. As Eyal Hareuveni observes, in a report written for the Israeli human rights organization B'tselem, most of the twenty-six Israeli nature reserves along the Jordan Valley and northern Dead Sea were previously closed military areas and today allow no access: "Israel forbids Palestinians to enter or remain there, whether to live or to graze their flocks." The difference between a closed military area and an Israeli nature reserve seems to me that reserves are often declared near sources of water.

"Won't you come inside? You are standing in thorns," said the young boy's mother, coming up the hill with an embarrassed gesture toward the tangled ground, as if she is responsible for the prickly land she inhabits. Her husband, the official recipient of donor largesse—in this case the plastic sheds—has gone to Toubas. The pleasant young man from the Ministry of Agriculture office in Toubas, who is accompanying us, says that she can answer our questions: "All the work is shared between the husband and the wife." Her answer to Intissaar's first question is diplomatic but pointed: "Oh, yes," she says, "we were happy to get the sheds." But then she adds: "but it would have been better to get them at the beginning of winter, it's too hot inside them for the animals now." Several sheep and one black goat are lying listlessly in the wadi; other animals have been moved inside the family's black tents. Smiling pleasantly, she offers this barbed observation and falls silent. Like the villagers in Al-Mughayyir, she is bewildered when asked who is the executing agency and who is the donor that provided the sheds for her flock. With a shy smile, she says that perhaps her husband would know.

Down the road and up a dirt track we find the larger household, or more accurately tenthold, of Abu Muhammed, an older man with what can only be described as an attitude. We definitely cannot refuse his invitation to enter his large black tent. We take off our shoes and sit on comfortable rugs and cushions, the only furnishings except for a battered standing cupboard with advertising stickers on it. Bags of feed are stored in the corner and a chicken manages to push her way under the tent flap and pecks contentedly as we discuss the fate of the seeds given to Abu Muhammed and his family. Abu Muhammed, like many Bedouins, has no passion for farming and says firmly that he would prefer to receive ready feed rather than seeds, which clearly are a hassle to plant in the stony landscape. He nonetheless requests more seeds: anything is better than nothing in this bleak environment. His flock numbers one hundred goats and sheep, a typical mixed herd for Bedouins, unlike the sheep-only villagers of Al-Mughayyir.

"What's your biggest problem?" I ask Abu Muhammed, and he answers in a word: "Water." This is perhaps an expected response in any of the arid regions of the Middle East, but there is more to it. The Toubas district itself is relatively fertile with a number of springs. With the help of the Palestine Hydrology Group, Abu Muhammed and other Bedouin herders had begun to construct water pools at a nearby spring by digging deeper into the spring's bed. In June 2016, the misnamed Planning and Construction Committee of Israel's Civil Administration ordered the work to be stopped. Ahmed, a neighbor and another seed beneficiary, added that their iron structures worth about 30,000 Israeli shekels (about $8,600) were taken away by the soldiers without any compensation. Yet another story in a chronology of confiscations, but this time I can hear the teller of his tale for myself. There is no complaint or entreaty in Ahmed's voice; he expects nothing.

Ahmed, like Abu Muhammed, says his family and tribe have come to the Jordan Valley from the Hebron Hills. About twenty thousand Bedouin live in Area C—half of all the Bedouins living in the occupied Palestinian territory according to the United Nations, and many have been forcibly relocated by the Israeli army more than one time. Indeed, most of the Bedouins living in Palestine originally came from the Naqab (Negev) Desert, now inside Israel, and were expelled or fled from there to the Hebron region in the course of the 1948 war and its aftermath. No one has ever traced the fate of all the animals that accompanied Bedouin and other Palestinian refugees on their long and dangerous treks to exile in 1948. Almost seven decades later, Ahmed, his family, and his flocks have been virtually immobilized on this patch of land where even the spring is under another's control. Ahmed's daughter, Mariam, a girl of perhaps ten years old, enters the tent, wearing a crisp pink dress with shiny accessories. She leans against Ahmed for a moment and then crosses the tent to greet us. She shyly offers her cheek for me to kiss.

As we drive back from the northern West Bank, our United Nations vehicle speeds past a man on a donkey leading his small herd of sheep and goats on the verge of the highway. I have often seen such small flocks, sometimes with a very young shepherd, in odd places along the road—under tunnels, near vacant lots, on top of abandoned cars, and in a narrow wedge of green beside the Wall in the village of Al-Walaja, near Jerusalem. Sometimes a shepherd and his flock venture near the outdoor cafés frequented by the young and well-off in Ramallah. But even in such close proximity to each other, the burgeoning Ramallah middle class and the declining shepherds live in distant worlds. Interaction is rare.

Ali, our driver, turns on the radio. All the news is bad, but the item recalling the attack, two days earlier, on Palm Sunday worshippers in two Coptic churches in Egypt is the worst. That Sunday morning, explosions, claimed by the Islamic State, ripped apart two congregations, killing forty-seven people. Ali, who is Muslim, lives on the Mount of Olives where the annual Palm Sunday procession sets out to follow Jesus's route into Jerusalem. Many Egyptian Coptic pilgrims, waving palm fronds, were among those who gathered to walk the steep path down to the Old City. As they assembled, media broadcast the news of the church explosions. Ali told me: "With my neighbors, we went out to the street to give them our condolences and share their grief." Pausing for a moment, he grips the steering wheel and says: "They were all poor people, why would anyone want to harm them?" Intissaar repeats his words softly.

When I ask the shepherds in Zanuta what keeps them there, given the lack of services and the looming threat of expulsion, Fayez answers that their life is "far away from urban problems," and Abu Hani repeats his mantra: "this land is our inheritance." Watching as another older man brings his small flock over a nearby knoll and the men look up at the widening sky to check the weather, I begin to see what Fayez means. The problems of goats and sheep seem simple compared to the problems of men and women.

CHAPTER 4

I WISH I WAS A DONKEY . . . OR DO I?

Mahmoud Darwish's image is compelling: A donkey patiently watches as humans in Palestine engage in bitter conflicts, cloud their lives with worries and tensions, and above all, labor under the weight of history (and in the case of those in occupied Palestine, under an unbearable present that must be borne.) A donkey's long view would seem most salutary.

But Darwish's malnourished donkey and his ancestors have, quite literally, carried the burden of history, as well as an equally heavy load of myth and metaphor. Those of his lineage famously bore Jesus into Jerusalem and Abraham up Mount Moriah; a relative is pictured watching over the infant Jesus in Bethlehem. Donkeys, second only to camels in their capacity to withstand heat and thirst, have plodded steadily in the innumerable caravans that crisscrossed the region, changing its human geography. These peaceful animals, alas, have also been requisitioned in war, including the two twentieth-century World Wars. In the long Israel–Palestine conflict, donkeys have occasionally become instruments of war themselves. In rural Palestine, they have endured the constant hard work of peasant life alongside their human companions, often sharing

Boys and a donkey riding through a spring pasture near Ramallah.
(Credit: Bassam Almohor)

the same dwellings and huddled together for warmth in harsh winters.

In the Israel Museum, a clay figure of a donkey bearing produce, excavated at the site of the city of Azor, on the coastal plain below Jaffa, is dated between 3500 and 3000 BCE. Five thousand years later, similar donkeys carrying similar goods trod the fields and streets of Yasur, the Palestinian Arab village that existed near the ruins of Azor until 1948 and that derived its name from the ancient city. The donkey (*Equus asinus*) has been part of Palestinian and Middle Eastern lives since its domestication in the Middle East from its Nubian wild ass ancestors in Africa sometime in the early Bronze Age. One of the great Middle Eastern cities, Damascus, was called by the ancient Assyrians the "city of asses" for the donkey caravans that congregated there. And one of the most illustrious, if infamous, queens of the region, Cleopatra, kept a stable of three hundred donkeys to provide her with milk for her beauty baths.

Almost two millennia later, when Mark Twain visited Palestine and the region, donkeys were still the means of transport during his caravan trip from Egypt to Palestine. The usually sarcastic author had nothing but praise for his sturdy companions and their Egyptian-style adornments, calling them "indescribably gorgeous." Among the white, black, and "mouse-colored" donkeys, "several of the white ones were barred like zebras with rainbow stripes of blue and red and yellow paint," while others were shaved in "fanciful garden-like patterns." He does not go on to describe the encounters of these gorgeous creatures with the utilitarian donkeys more common in Palestine, but we can imagine a moment of donkey astonishment.

"Where are all the donkeys?" my observant neighbor Vera

asked one spring day in the late 1990s. When I first arrived in Ramallah fifteen years before, donkeys in the city were harbingers of spring, brought into town, along with mules, to plow under the olive and fruit trees in household gardens and to transport people and produce from neighboring villages to town. I used to wake each spring morning to the loud braying of a donkey tied to a tree in my landlord's large garden. But Vera was right: the donkeys had largely vanished from springtime Ramallah. In a global age of post-domesticity—with many people and most in Europe and North America having little or no contact with working or productive animals—what has happened to the donkeys of Palestine?

My nephew Aziz, who has just turned twenty, tells me he does not remember encountering a donkey in Ramallah's streets. Donkeys may have been decommissioned from their urban responsibilities in Ramallah, although not in all Palestinian towns by a long shot. They are still key working animals for small farmers and herders, especially in remote communities, as well as for Bedouin communities in the hills of the southern West Bank and the arid stretches of the Jerusalem wilderness. Driving from the Ramallah hills down to the Jordan Valley—below sea level—in the spring of 2017, the stony slopes, graced with fleeting tufts of green, hosted twelve Bedouin encampments that I could spy from the road, each with a donkey or two standing, as if on guard, near the flocks of black goats and dusty sheep.

A lack of acquaintance with the animal does not stop Aziz from occasionally addressing annoying friends with a familiar epithet. *Hmaar!* (Donkey!) *Hmaar!*, muttered the middle-aged man standing in front of me in the long line at the Qalandia checkpoint, as an Israeli soldier turned away to play with his cellphone, leaving us in the hot sun. *Hmaar!*, a child hurls the

word in a playground scrap, as does a hardworking taxi driver
in a Ramallah traffic jam when a young driver in a BMW reck-
lessly cuts across the lane, music blaring. While the donkey
bears these associations of obstinacy and stupidity in other
parts of the world, including all the verbal offshoots of its less
elegant appellation *ass*, people seem to have more occasion to
call each other donkey amid the tensions of life in Palestine/
Israel.

"Look, that's where it was," said George Al-Ama, a Bethlehem art expert, as we drove by a wall with a deliberate rect-
angular chunk missing. Banksy, the world-famous street artist,
had painted *Donkey Documents* on that gray concrete surface
in 2007 during his second visit to Bethlehem. The image
was striking: an Israeli soldier in full gear stops a donkey and
checks his documents. A previous appearance of a Bansky donkey in Bethlehem in 2005 had garnered mixed local reviews:
the donkey, as well as Bansky's iconic rat (posed with a sling-
shot), had met with protest from some Bethlehemites: "It gives
the impression that we are donkeys," complained one former
Bethlehem official.

I look at the indentation: Where are the soldier and donkey
now?

Bethlehem, a site of pilgrimage for two thousand years, is
the Palestinian city most affected by the Wall that not only
cuts it off from Jerusalem—only a few miles away—but erodes
local livelihoods and prospects for the city's future. Banksy
was determined to make the chilling gray cement surface of
the Wall a canvas to protest against itself. In December 2007,
he brought twenty-five European and American artists to the
beleaguered city to create *Santa's Ghetto*. They created art on
the Wall and art for sale to raise funds for Bethlehem. In one
famous Banksy image, a dove carries an olive branch in its

beak but wears a bulletproof vest: cross hairs are etched on the dove's heart.

More than ten years later, George is our guide on the trail of the fate of Banksy's *Donkey Documents*. George is a Bethlehemite to his core; he began his career learning about, and trading in, religious icons and is currently deeply involved in both the collecting of Palestinian art and the preservation of the historic treasures of the city. We drive by Bansky's incandescent dove, delighted it is still there. But our donkey has departed, leaving only a chalky white space with a few ghostly graffiti from the two Palestinian intifadas still visible. Many of Bansky's original images have vanished, either painted over by other graffiti artists or, in one case, by a menu from a local restaurant. Bethlehem has been a town that has traded in artifacts, from icons and elaborate mother of pearl items to tawdry tourist gimmicks, for a very long time; some residents began to realize that valuable contemporary icons were painted on Bethlehem's concrete Wall.

Among them was *Donkey Documents*, which Banksy spray-painted not on the Wall itself, but on a less intimidating, but obviously tempting, nearby wall that was topped by a concrete shack and adjacent to one of Bethlehem's souvenir shops. The owner, George explained, knew what he had—almost—in his grasp and moved to secure possession of the concrete surface hosting a work by one of the world's leading street artists. And then one day, a truck pulled up and *Donkey Documents* was carefully cut out of the wall and hauled away. The owner had sold it.

I was alerted to its fate when I read an announcement from Julien's Auctions in Los Angeles. An autumn 2015 auction of "street art" would include two important works by Bansky. One was *Donkey Documents*, described as "aerosol on a composite stone wall" with an asking price, much reported in the press, of $600,000. Potential buyers were assured that the present owner had legally purchased the piece from the owners of the Bethlehem building. Banksy's donkey seemed poised to become one of the most valuable donkeys of all time. To be sure, donkeys have been portrayed by other, older Masters, but generally not in the title role; they are minor, rather than central images. Bellini's painting *Saint Francis in the Desert*, in The Frick Collection in New York, has a donkey peacefully standing in the background looking at the enraptured saint, who does not return his gaze. Jan Brueghel the Elder's wonderful *Adam and Eve in the Garden of Eden* portrays a harmonious Golden Age: a leopard and ox play together in the painting's foreground, while Adam and Eve are distant background figures. On the side, two small donkeys ignore the cavorting animals and do what they do best, graze peacefully. In contemporary Palestine, Khaled Hourani captured an odd moment in donkey adornment in *The Zebra Copy Card*. Hourani celebrated Gaza zoo owner Nidal Barghouti's own artistic intervention when he painted black zebra stripes on white donkeys to entertain children in one of Gaza's bereft zoos.

In Los Angeles, no one stepped forward to purchase *Donkey Documents*; the auction site simply noted "lot closed—remains unsold." The other work by Banksy, cut from the wall of an abandoned Packard factory in Detroit, promptly found a bidder. Do street art collectors also have donkey prejudices, or is it the raw nerve of Israel/Palestine politics that deterred buyers? I ask George whether there is any chance that our donkey could be returned to Bethlehem. "So difficult," he says, noting the lack of both resources and political clout. But the residents of Bethlehem and the crippled Palestinian Authority have acted to save the remaining works of Banksy. When Bethlehem witnessed another attempt to remove an important Banksy in 2015—a young Palestinian girl frisking a soldier, a pleasant contrast to the soldier–donkey confrontation in *Donkey Documents*—Bethlemites alerted the Palestinian Police, who managed to stop the removal. Then, Palestine's Ministry of Tourism issued an edict declaring all remaining works of Banksy in Palestine "national treasures"; tampering with them became illegal. Too late for *Donkey Documents*, but a sign of hope. In the nearby town of Beit Sahur, a large Bansky mural of a young Palestinian man masked with a keffiyeh and throwing a bouquet of flowers, rather than the more usual stones, still stands next to a gas station.

A small replica of *Donkey Documents* has its place in Banksy's latest Bethlehem project, where we ended our investigation that day. *The Walled Off Hotel*—its installation planned and paid for by Banksy and then turned over to local operators—opened in March 2017, attractively advertising the "worst view in the world." It stands next to the Wall and hosts a colonial-style tea room where a life-size puppet of the British Foreign Secretary, Lord Balfour, continually signs the 1917 Balfour Declaration. In the small but evocative museum, replete with photo collages of resistance to the Wall, as well as maps and statistics, there is a photo of *Donkey Documents*. The caption does not mention its journey to Los Angeles but simply notes that some Palestinians found the image offensive.

Donkeys evoke more positive, even intimate, feelings among their peasant and Bedouin owners. Memories of growing up with a family donkey are almost always pleasant. My sociologist friend Jamil Hilal, now in his seventies, recalled many enjoyable rides on his uncle's donkey on the outskirts of Beit Sahur, near Bethlehem. Bassam Almohor, a generation or so younger and a photographer-companion on many a walk, grew up in a village in the northern West Bank and regularly rode the family donkey, Aziza, to help out in the fields or simply to get around. *Aziza* means darling in Arabic and is a common name for favorite working animals, when they are named at all. One day, nine-year-old Bassam was riding Aziza in the wheat field just after harvest when he became mesmerized by her long, flapping ears. He had at hand a pair of locking pliers and, in a disastrous fit of high spirits, attached them to Aziza's ear. Aziza promptly threw him off. Bassam had tied the donkey's rope around his waist and was dragged ignominiously through the sharp stubble. To top it off, his father beat Bassam to teach him a lesson: never mistreat the donkey. Fortunately for Bassam, donkeys are more forgiving than camels, which are human-like in their ability to hold a grudge and exact revenge. Bassam continued to ride his chosen form of transport.

A child enjoying a donkey ride is certainly not unique to a Palestinian setting. However, some human–donkey partnerships can only belong to Palestine and to a very particular moment. It was February 1987; the First Palestinian Intifada with its mass nonviolent resistance would erupt at the end of that tumultuous year. That day, shopkeepers in Ramallah were on strike, and Birzeit University historian Roger Heacock was scouring the Ramallah streets for an open store where he could purchase juice for his sick child. Diverted by a group of women protesting the treatment of Palestinian refugees in Lebanon, he went to see their signs and was promptly arrested by an Israeli soldier for leading a women's demonstration. The soldier shouted at Roger, "You did this." This Israeli was obviously not in tune with the very active Palestinian women's movement, whose members might appreciate Roger's solidarity but certainly did not need his leadership.

Nonetheless, Roger was in trouble. In pursuit, I went with his wife Laura, pushing her infant son Jamal (of juice fame) in a baby carriage, to try to find our prisoner in the Ramallah police station, then under the control of the Israeli occupation, although Palestinian policemen filled the lower ranks. Entering its dank unsanitary corridor, we spied Roger among other prisoners in a small holding cell under the stairs of this Ottoman-era building. Roger could only wave at us from his barred cell. Four months later, Roger was finally released when the judge in military court sentenced him to time already served in prison after declaring that he did not believe any of the stream of defense and character witnesses. Raja, who was Roger's lawyer, swore to never again take a case to military court.

Over a gin and tonic, I recently asked Roger to remind us of his time behind bars. He had been spared the ritual welcome of being beaten up by his cellmates when the policeman escorting him, a Palestinian employee of the Israeli system, used the language of Palestinian resistance to warn the other detainees off Roger: "Don't hurt him. He is a nationalist struggler." His attitude to Roger was a good indicator of the next action taken by the Palestinian police employed by Israel in the Occupied Territories: their mass resignation during the intifada a year later.

Amid several other surreal tales of his imprisonment, Roger told us about a Palestinian thief and his donkey. Roger explained that the next prisoner who tumbled in the cell after Roger did receive the customary beating from his fellows, after which embraces cemented the new relationship. Roger was drawn to the man, who was deaf and could hardly speak. His story came out in bits and pieces, aided by the Palestinian tea server who cheerfully acknowledged himself as a police spy, called an *asfour* (bird) in Arabic. "The guy entered a minimarket near Ramallah with his donkey and robbed it of some cigarettes," Roger recalled, barely containing his mirth. "But the thing was he disguised his donkey—wrapping a Palestinian checkered keffiyeh around his head—but forgot to hide his own face." The man was later arrested in the center of Ramallah peddling the cigarettes, his accomplice donkey beside him. The donkey was spared detention.

Donkey–human partnerships take many forms, fortunately not all of them criminal. One autumn morning in 2007, we sat under an olive tree as our walking group stopped for a picnic in the Ramallah hills. With a mischievous smile, Samia Al-Botmeh, a professor of economics at Birzeit University and a dedicated hiker, told me the story of her aunt's donkey. Samia is from Battir, a village near Bethlehem, whose ancient olive terraces (one suspects the stones were hauled by donkeys) were recently declared a World Heritage Site. As a child, Samia woke up to the braying of donkeys, including her aunt's female donkey, who competed noisily with other Battir donkeys—the bray of a donkey can be heard from two miles away. In Battir, Samia remarked, peasants did not name their donkeys, but nonetheless, her aunt's donkey had quite a story.

Samia's aunt worked on her land as a "traditional peasant." She had purchased her donkey from a woman in the village who was selling her because she was unruly. With some effort, the aunt managed to control the sprightly creature. "At first," Samia told me, "the donkey was simply her car," carrying her up the steep hills of Battir to her orchards and fields. But as Samia's aunt aged, the donkey grew into her closest companion. When urged to visit her nieces in Ramallah, she always refused, telling Samia, "the donkey would be lonely without me."

But then there was a dramatic development: Samia's brother Jawad was getting married in London. A former prisoner, he could not return to Palestine. "My aunt left the donkey and traveled with us. We visited many sites in London and she never uttered a word about her new surroundings. She only insisted that we telephone her nephew in Battir every day to inquire about the donkey." But then, when the family was walking in Hyde Park, Samia's aunt finally spoke: "If only the donkey was here," she said, "she would have enjoyed all this greenery."

The story is comic but also poignant for its glimpse into a rural way of life that may be vanishing, and doubly so because Jawad is unlikely to ever see his village home again. While Jawad's troubles are beyond my remit, I began to explore how donkeys still contribute to the difficult struggle for a livelihood among marginalized communities, whether Bedouin encampments or remote villages. On a winter walk on the bleak eastern slopes near Ramallah that reach down to the Jordan Valley, a shepherd rides past on a donkey and I see a small head emerging from his saddlebags: a newborn goat who couldn't keep up with the herd. The donkey remains a reliable "car" for man and beast in this stony landscape.

Donkeys come in particularly handy in Area C, that unfortunate 61 percent of the West Bank under direct Israeli control. Of great significance to the Palestinian farmers and villagers living there, Area C is the locus not just of Israeli military bases but of more than one hundred Israeli settlements established in the West Bank since 1967, in violation of international law, specifically the Fourth Geneva Convention. The Palestinian village of Al-Khader is near Bethlehem but nearer still to the massive Gush Etzion settlement bloc. In better times, both Christians and Muslims congregated in the village for a festival at the shrine of Al-Khader or Saint George, the fourth-century Christian martyr. Now, villagers in Al-Khader have trouble getting to their own fields. One farmer, Ibrahim Abu

Mousa, told a Palestinian news agency in 2015: "I travel tens of kilometers back and forth on the back of my donkey to access my land near Gush Etzion." Under the frequently used rubric of security, Israel had closed the agricultural roads that led to his fields, which abut the settlement. Thus a donkey was called once more into service. While donkeys are not the usual means of transport on modern four-lane highways, they can often be seen plodding along on the southern West Bank's busy Route 60 as farmers attempt to get to their orchards on the other side of the road. On February 8, 2017, an elderly man from Al-Khader riding on his donkey was hit and killed by a minibus driven by a settler who fled the scene.

Whether settler or soldier, the Israeli occupation continues to collide with the lives of donkeys. In August 2016, an unusual advertisement appeared in the local Arabic press: the Israeli army advertised "forty donkeys for sale." While the Israeli authorities claim they round up wandering livestock to reduce road accidents, farmers in Area C tell a different story: of soldiers, and sometimes settlers, seizing their animals, whether donkeys, sheep, or goats; of heavy fines imposed on poor villagers; of agricultural land turned into army training grounds. Settler intervention can be lethal. In 2008 a shepherd from the village of Burin in the northern West Bank reported settlers from nearby Har Bracha firing on his flock, killing a donkey and four sheep.

Donkeys, as well as horses and mules, have been involved in human conflicts since the time of their domestication. Donkeys' strength, stamina, and cheap upkeep, as well as their ability to navigate difficult and rocky terrain, have made them a military asset since the Syrians used them to pull war carts in the early Bronze Age. These long-enduring creatures were present in the trenches of World War I, usually as pack animals, and labored most famously at the bloody battle of Gallipoli, where fierce Ottoman resistance defeated a land invasion from British, French, Australian, and New Zealand forces. At Gallipoli, on present-day Turkey's coast, donkeys, wearing Red Cross headbands, carried water to the wounded and transported them to safety. An Australian stretcher bearer, John Simpson, and his donkey rescued about three hundred soldiers before Simpson was killed.

On World War I's Palestinian front, donkeys carried supplies to the troops, particularly water, and transported the injured. In World War II, donkeys also served, but with less arduous duties. A postcard photograph sent by an Australian soldier stationed in southern Palestine during World War II shows a donkey dressed in regulation striped pajamas with a slouched Australian hat on his head. For the soldiers, it was a moment of relaxation and comic relief; the sentiments of the donkey remain unknown, but it was at least a break from battlefield duties and dangers.

Then, in 2003—in the throes of the second violence-ridden Palestinian intifada—a donkey was once again pressed into wartime service. This time the consequences were lethal. In February of that catastrophic year in Palestine and Israel, Ingrid Newkirk, the president of People for the Ethical Treatment of Animals (PETA), a major international animal welfare organization, wrote Palestinian President Yasser Arafat to protest an incident where Palestinian militants from the Hamas movement had detonated explosives packed onto a donkey near a Jerusalem bus stop. The sole victim was the donkey. The PETA letter asked Arafat to "appeal to all those who listen to you to leave animals out of the conflict." At the time of the letter, Arafat himself was under siege in his headquarters in Ramallah, the Muqata, surrounded by Israeli tanks and unable to command much beyond the confines of his bunker. I recently visited that underground bunker, now preserved as a key element of the Arafat Museum: his office contained only a plain desk, a few chairs, and, touchingly, a poster of Rachel Corrie, the American activist crushed to death by an Israeli bulldozer in March 2003, when she tried to prevent the demolition of a Palestinian home in Gaza.

I asked a friend who was Arafat's translator at the time if she thought he received the letter—postal services to his bunker being somewhat unreliable—and her answer was probably not. When the letter was made public, it aroused a storm of protest among pro-Israeli commentators, who berated PETA for considering a donkey over the Israeli victims of the conflict. In besieged Palestine, it passed unnoticed. When, more than a decade later, I told the story of the PETA letter to my nephew Aziz—always a sounding board for me—his first reaction was incredulous laughter: "I told the story to all my friends," he reported later. "They couldn't believe it."

It is not that Aziz is hard-hearted; he is one of the kindest and most thoughtful young men I know. But he was six years old in the spring of 2002 when the Israeli army invaded Ramallah, the year before PETA intervened on behalf of donkeys. On March 29, 2002, Israel launched Operation Protective Shield, the largest military operation since 1967, citing "self-defense" after a March 27 suicide bombing at the Park Hotel in the coastal city of Netanya killed nineteen Israelis. The young bomber was from the West Bank town of Tulkarem, only ten miles away from Netanya. In better days, Tulkarem residents used to come to Netanya to enjoy a day at the beach. The Park Hotel bombing was claimed by the military wing of Hamas and may have been aimed at disrupting the ceasefire being proposed at the time in an Arab League peace initiative.

And indeed there was no ceasefire. Ramallah was placed under curfew as two hundred Israeli tanks rumbled down the city streets, crushing parked cars and threatening any unwary resident that had not found shelter. One tank parked near the apartment where Aziz lived with his parents, Samer and Hanan, and his younger sister, Tala. Soldiers broke in through the kitchen window, occupied the building, and forced the upstairs neighbors to come down to the family's apartment, locking everyone into three rooms. Tala was fearful but too young to fully understand. She whispered to her mother "Turkey is nice," hinting that she would rather be where the family had spent a pleasant beach vacation the previous summer. But Aziz watched as his father was taken away at gunpoint to act as a human shield. Upon his return, Samer managed to call Raja and whispered for help; soldiers had ordered him not to use his phone. Raja called the US Consulate—the whole family are US citizens—to get the simple response: "We can do nothing." The soldiers stayed for four long days and nights. Under curfew half a mile away in our house, I looked out the window a few days later to find the International Committee of the Red Cross collecting the garbage; its international humanitarian mandate and its duties under international law had been reduced to waste disposal.

Aziz's own traumatic experience perhaps explains his incredulity at PETA's initiative to save the lives of donkeys. I am haunted by an innocent donkey bearing lethal explosives, but I am even more deeply troubled by the inattention to human life. It is hard also not to recall a long history of colonial officials—particularly those of the British Empire—reacting more strongly to the abuse of animals than of the colonized humans that surrounded them. Lord Cromer, who governed Egypt for the British Empire, was both a strong believer in Britain's colonial mission, with its assumptions of the inferiority of native Egyptians, particularly peasants, and an equally staunch advocate of animal welfare, a patron of the first society for the prevention of cruelty to animals in Cairo, at the end of the nineteenth century.

The unfortunate donkey dispatched by Hamas in 2003 was not the first of its kind to be used as an instrument of war in the conflict over Palestine. In 1939, an explosive-laden donkey was sent into a Haifa marketplace by the Irgun, a Zionist militia. Twenty-seven Arabs were killed. And the same years in which PETA protested the death of a small gray donkey witnessed other acts of animal cruelty that went largely unnoticed. In August 2001, Israeli settlers from the settlement of Itamar, known for their extremism, slaughtered a pasture full of sheep belonging to the villagers of Yanun. The effects of this and other attacks by Itamar settlers were dire; villagers began to flee Yanun, which was on its way to becoming the first Palestinian village abandoned by its inhabitants since 1948. When I visited Yanun three years later, villagers still received fearsome harassment but were resolved to stay put. As we walked through the village we encountered a young Italian woman chatting with two young Palestinian girls: she told us she was an international volunteer trying to help the people of Yanun to remain. International solidarity and human rights groups had established a permanent presence in the village. I watched a young boy and a donkey pick their way up a steep path, the donkey occasionally pausing for a nibble at the green verge. A moment of peace.

The question of whose lives are valued and how human and animal rights and welfare might be intertwined looms large not only over me but also the relatively new Palestinian animal welfare and wildlife conservation organizations and activists that have emerged in the last decade or so. Interestingly, at present there are not one but two initiatives from local Palestinian NGOs to promote donkey welfare—the Palestinian Animal League, founded in 2011 under the telling slogan "Helping Animals, Empowering People," and the older Palestine Wildlife Society, founded in 1998 in the southern West Bank. Both donkey projects work with villagers and their animals and both are partially supported by donkey welfare organizations in the United Kingdom, an intriguing partnership emerging from a troubled colonial history.

"People genuinely think donkeys are hardier than other animals and don't need as much water and food," Ahmad Safi of the Palestinian Animal League (PAL) told me as we sat in a Ramallah café, his phone buzzing with messages about the League's new vegan café at Al-Quds (Jerusalem) University. He told me about PAL's experience working with young Bedouin men and boys, whose donkeys bear tourists down the long ravine of Wadi Qelt, where the cliff-hanging monastery of Saint George is located. Saint George, the same holy man whose shrine is worshipped in Al-Khader, is omnipresent in Palestine. "When our volunteers first went to Wadi Qelt they found donkeys tied in the hot sun with no water and food." After discussions with PAL volunteers, the donkey owners, teenagers for the most part, took only a few months to begin providing their animals with constant water and food. But they could not provide shade: the Bedouin of Wadi Qelt are forbidden from growing trees or erecting a canopy against the unrelenting heat: the whole area, stretching from Ein Farah, the upper spring of the wadi near Jerusalem, to Jericho, below sea level, has been declared a nature reserve, a move that might be welcome if it were not a code word for Area C. Ahmad told me that the security guard from a nearby settlement had recently destroyed a Bedouin tent near Wadi Qelt and soldiers had leveled six Bedouin shacks. In the midst of all these human problems, PAL was still able to convince the young donkey owners to replace painful iron bridles with soft cotton or plastic harnesses. "People also believe donkeys are headstrong," commented Ahmad, "but these bridles were completely unnecessary."

Young Bedouins are not the only people to misconstrue donkey behavior. It is in donkey nature to be cautious: donkeys weigh the dangers when new experiences confront them and can balk at an unacceptable risk. Frustrating perhaps for an impatient owner, but donkeys' careful behavior can be a godsend for those seeking paths through the stony wilderness of the eastern slopes. "See that road you came on," Imad Atrash of the Palestine Wildlife Society told me, as we looked down from his office window at the Wadi Nar (Valley of Fire) road that twists up the canyons of the Jerusalem wilderness toward Beit Sahur and Bethlehem. "The road-makers followed the paths made by donkeys."

An old adage offers the advice: "You tell a horse what to do, ask a donkey, and negotiate with a mule." Those who do not follow this wisdom may run into difficulties. Consider Robert Louis Stevenson's frustrations with his stubborn donkey companion, Modestine, during the hike through Southern France he describes in his *Travels with a Donkey in the Cévennes*. Modestine, Stevenson wrote, exhausted his spirit until he gave up and walked the entire journey at her slow pace. But even Modestine was a somewhat easier companion than the recalcitrant donkey companion of Ziauddin Sardar, the author of a recent history of the ancient city of Mecca, critical of the deleterious changes wrought by the Saudi regime in that holy city. In the 1990s, Sardar decided to follow in the footsteps of his hero, the fourteenth-century chronicler and traveler Ibn Battuta, who set out from Tangiers on a pilgrimage to Mecca, accompanied by a donkey. Sardar planned a shorter haj (pilgrimage) from Jeddah on the Red Sea to Mecca, with his newly acquired donkey, aptly named Genghis. In their slow progress, Genghis was more interested in fleeing to romance other donkeys than trudging along with his human companions. Genghis was eventually sent on to Mecca in a pickup truck while Ziauddin and his friend Zafar continued on foot. Reunited on the outskirts of Mecca, Genghis apparently decided to be a five-star traveler and escaped into the lobby of the Intercontinental Hotel. When Zardar attempted to persuade the staff that it was the pilgrimage season and time to show love to all creation, the head porter replied curtly, "You love the donkey if you want to. But do it outside the hotel."

Sometimes donkeys and people click. Writer Andy Merrifield found tranquility in a chaotic world as he accompanied a chocolate-colored donkey named Gribouille on a slow (donkey pace) journey through southern France. Merrifield let Gribouille chose the path, although he and Gribouille did engage in negotiations over grazing time: "we can't stop *all the time* for him to eat." Their growing relationship has the ring of the tender intimacy between Sancho Panza and his donkey, Dapple, in *Don Quixote*. Sancho Panza called his small gray donkey "the delight of his eyes" and a "dearest companion" in the topsy-turvy world Sancho and Don Quixote inhabited. Looking at the fractured Spain of the early seventeenth century and our conflicted Palestine today, perhaps we still need the comfort of donkey companions as much as ever.

Modestine and Gribouille differ in temperament, and Genghis was in a class of his own. And while Ahmad was more than right in his emphasis on improved care for the hardworking donkeys of Wadi Qelt, it is true, at least by human standards, that donkeys measure up as hardy. Donkeys can withstand high degrees of dehydration, rehydrate quite quickly, and carry heavy loads for their size. And while perhaps not headstrong, donkeys are clearly committed to self-preservation. But even while reflecting on donkey traits as recorded by humans, I wonder whether this most familiar of animals, a constant companion and working animal over thousands of years, is perhaps also surprisingly strange to us. Is a donkey truly known to us—and us to it?

It can be hard to catch a donkey's gaze, which is often downcast, with the animal using his or her long ears to express fear, anger, or plain old contentment. But standing in a rocky field, I try. I see a small brown donkey with a sore spot on its flank: it raises its head and looks at me. I consider John Berger's observation that humans and animals scrutinize each other over a "narrow abyss of non-comprehension." I can tick off my list of donkey characteristics, but there is something important I do not know: what the donkey sees in me. A famous question asked by the sixteenth-century essayist Michel de Montaigne comes to mind: "Am I playing with my cat or is my cat playing with me?" A cat has often been called a "familiar," in the sense of a spirit—or indeed minor demon—that accompanies a witch as a helper. But donkeys are fated to be more ordinary "familiars" for us run-of-the-mill humans who need, I think, their companionship. On the outskirts of the bustling southern West Bank town of Dhahiriya, its shops displaying bright, Bedouin-style clothing and its only street congested on a busy afternoon, I spy two boys riding a white donkey up toward an orchard: bareback, their thin legs clutch the donkey's rounded belly. It is a moment of contentment. Something in the exchange between a human and an animal feels differ-

ent from our encounters with each other: in the words of John
Berger again, it is a "companionship offered to the loneliness
of man as a species."

Species loneliness: this strikes a profound chord in a world
in which wild animals are vanishing at an accelerating rate and
where humans seek alien intelligence in the universe but sever
their connection with their closest species companions. Here,
many would cite chimpanzees, as we are largely constituted of
the same DNA with only a 4 percent variation. But we share a
long (and more intimate) working history with other animals.
These working animals offer us an interaction that we often
take for granted. With the heartbreaking urgency of initiatives
to save wild animals faced with habitat loss and extinction, it is
easy to forget these constant companions in both their famil-
iarity and their strangeness.

I consider other mysterious aspects of donkeys as I watch
goats, sheep, and several dogs follow a donkey up a scrabbly
hill in the Jordan Valley. Donkeys, as far as I know, don't like
dogs—and in some countries are even used to guard flocks
against stray dogs—so why this everyday interaction? "Why
do dogs and goats follow donkeys?" I ask my veterinarian
friend Amro. He provides an answer: a young male goat kid
is taken away from his mother immediately and fed donkey
milk and then tied to the donkey. Then, castrated and usually
with a bell around his neck, he will follow the donkey and lead
the rest of the flock. Similarly, a puppy is tied to the donkey
and fed her milk, which creates a shared bond. These shepherd practices are embedded in a long tradition. In Dublin's
National Gallery of Ireland, I stand, intrigued, before *Caravan
on the Nile*, a painting by the nineteenth-century French artist
Jean-Léon Gérôme. A donkey and her rider, her foal tied by a
rope to her saddle, lead a long procession of goats, camels, and

their riders along a curve in the majestic river. The donkey looks straight at the viewer. An orientalist-inflected vision, but Gérôme's entirely realistic donkey wins me over: donkeys are clearly guides a goat, camel, or human can trust.

My human-donkey romanticism is undercut by Ahmad's more hardscrabble view of the relations between donkeys and their impoverished Palestinian owners. He explained how the cost of caring for animals, including donkeys, makes people resort to traditional remedies that can be harmful, giving examples of herders treating their donkeys' infections by burning them, which kills the nerves, and treating their skin disease with motor oil. Volunteer vets who are graduates of the new School of Veterinary Medicine at An-Najah University are working at present with farmers and herders to explain why these practices hurt the animals and to find better solutions. It is not always easy when household resources are so limited. One Bedouin told Ahmad: "When my child is ill, I give him herbs and keep him warm, should I take my donkey to the doctor?"

I had been harassing Ahmad by email to let me accompany PAL on a field visit with one of the volunteer vets to explore some of these issues. But the course of a Palestinian non-governmental organization never runs smooth, and the roads in the West Bank that must be traversed present their own obstacles. So I was delighted when Murad, a PAL volunteer and An-Najah University graduate, sent a message inviting me to come along on a field visit one Saturday in May, his day off from his job with the Ministry of Agriculture in Hebron. But I was somewhat crestfallen to learn his destination: the new riding club at Rawabi. Rawabi, rising on a lovely hill north of Ramallah, is the first Palestinian planned city—and alas, its first gated community. Slated to accommodate largely middle-class families and built with massive investment from

Qatar and support from international donors, Rawabi can stir uncomfortable feelings in any leftist heart or indeed in anyone who looks back to times when there was much less inequality and class division in occupied Palestine. In Rawabi, both donkeys and their peasant and Bedouin owners would be an anachronism.

Surprisingly, I found I was not alone in my stirrings of class resentment. Abu Ali, the head of the riding school, angrily puts down the phone as we enter the temporary hut that is his office. "I won't do it," he exclaims. A handsome and powerful man, he is upset with the administration of Rawabi, which is demanding he raise his fees. "I don't serve one class," he tells us. "I want to do something for all of Palestine." It may seem surprising to find class analysis uttered by the head of a riding school, but this is Palestine, and politics are in the bones. Abu Ali and his team, all originally from Jericho, previously ran the popular riding school in Turmus Aya, a village on the road to Nablus made prosperous by the many residents sending remittances from work abroad. Recently, one such resident decided to sell the land of the riding school and thus, a few months ago, Abu Ali moved to Rawabi. He now wants to leave. His commitment to Palestine is through his horses: "Take this one. She is already twenty-three years old, but the young children love her. If I can take good care of her and establish a small horse hospital, she might live to be the oldest horse in the world—a record for Palestine!" In the stalls, however, Murad is upset that the staff is not taking proper care of a horse with an infected leg. The mood is dispirited and a few months later, the riding school closes its doors. If Rawabi is not a healthy environment for horses, what does it say for its human inhabitants and the new Palestinian city on a hill it symbolizes?

Life is also changing in Ramallah, and at least for its young professional class, trendy cafés are more on the mind than the welfare of donkeys and other animals. But a touch of donkey nostalgia hangs in the air. Raja's cousin Nadim now organizes a spring donkey ride in the fertile valley below Ramallah, where the village of Ein Kenya is nestled, named for its welcoming spring. A few years after the establishment of the Palestinian Authority, we hiked to the spring and noticed several donkeys resting in the shade of trees. "They are in retirement," Raja noted. Donkeys had been the hard-worked pack animals that brought water from the spring to the village, but finally, in 1997, the village was connected to the water network. The donkeys may have retired then, I thought, but now, it seems, they have been repurposed. Farmers still work them at harvest time, but each spring, they bring them to Nadim's donkey ride: in 2016, owners brought sixty donkeys from Ein Kenya and surrounding villages to delight about one hundred children and their parents.

Donkeys will, I think, endure in Palestine, whether guiding flocks in the Jerusalem wilderness or entertaining children on a spring morning. Their ancestors, however, Syrian wild asses, were yet another casualty of World War I, becoming extinct in the wake of widespread hunting after Lawrence of Arabia distributed hundreds of thousands of rifles to Bedouins and other Arabs to encourage rebellion against the Ottomans. In yet another twist, in 1968 an Israeli general acquired three pairs of Persian wild asses from the Shah of Iran in exchange for twenty deer. He housed them in the Naqab (Negev) Desert, hoping to reintroduce a "Biblical" species to an ancient land. In the absence of predators and the presence of tasty Negev agriculture, they thrived and are currently perceived as a menace both to desert wild plants in the high hills of the Negev and to farmers' vineyards and fields. "Everything was green, now there's only dust," one resident told an Israeli newspaper.

Samia's aunt, as she grew older and infirm, realized one day that she could no longer take care of her beloved donkey. "Take her to the zoo," she asked Samia. The Jerusalem Biblical Zoo is just across the Wall that today separates Battir from Jerusalem, and Samia's aunt had memories of seeing the well-cared-for animals in better days when visits to that Israeli-run zoo were part of Battir's world. In 2015, children in Battir instead marked the anniversary of the fall of the Berlin Wall by flying white balloons over the shuttered train station and over the Wall beyond. Their message was "From Battir to Berlin," and their hope was for another Wall to fall.

Samia is highly competent, and even under current restrictions, the donkey, according to the aunt's wishes, was delivered to the zoo with the help of a neighbor. What she didn't tell her aunt was that all old donkeys, whether at the Jerusalem zoo or its beleaguered cousin in Qalqilya, meet the same fate. As Dr. Sami in Qalqilya told me: "Farmers give me their old donkeys. I put them to sleep as painlessly as I can. Then I feed them to the lions." Ecologically sound, perhaps, but still a sad fate for a cherished donkey whose owner dreamed one day might blissfully walk in the green of Hyde Park.

CHAPTER 5

WHERE ARE WE GOING, RIVKA?: COWS IN AN OCCUPIED ECONOMY

"Where are we going, Rivka?" asks a plaintive animated cow in a recent film, *The Wanted 18*, as she rattles along on an illegal journey from Israel to the West Bank Palestinian town of Beit Sahur in 1988. Beit Sahur residents, in the throes of a mass civil disobedience campaign during the First Palestinian Intifada against the Israeli occupation, had decided that they did not want to be dependent on Tnuva, the Israeli dairy giant, and had bought eighteen nervous cows from a sympathetic Israeli kibbutz. Amer Shomali and Paul Cowan's remarkable 2014 film chronicles the true story of the "wanted eighteen" as Amer conducts interviews with both the Israeli military officials who dispatched soldiers to round up the "illegal" cows and the Palestinians from Beit Sahur who played an almost nightly game of hide-and-seek with armed soldiers.

Shomali's animated cows are more than doubtful about their new home: "I don't want to have my baby in the desert," one cow sobs during their long ride, while another opines that Palestinians only throw stones and never work. Indeed, the Palestinians of Beit Sahur, according to an eyewitness account by my Birzeit University colleague Ghassan Andoni, definitely lacked cow competence: when the real eighteen cows arrived

Cows wanted by the Israeli military carry the Palestinian flag on a hill near Beit Sahur. *(Credit: Amer Shomali and Paul Cowan)*

in the town, they promptly escaped from the truck while Beit Sahur's doctors, engineers, pharmacists, and business people futilely tried to corral them. Fortunately, several Bedouin neighbors, adept at rounding up livestock, came to the rescue.

Beit Sahur's initiative to raise cows was part of a range of intifada-era community activities—from home gardens to the education of students—propelled by the (illegal of course) neighborhood committees. All 1,194 schools in the West Bank, including kindergartens, were closed by military order in February 1988; all six Palestinian universities had received closure orders by January 1988. Raja's affable brother, Samer, was the popular head of the agricultural committee in his middle-class Ramallah neighborhood and enjoyed inspecting the tiny shoots in household gardens even though his skills at plant identification and his ability to give useful advice were somewhat minimal. Beit Sahuris, who have a reputation for stubbornness, decided to go much further and launched the one and only Palestinian tax revolt, refusing to pay any taxes to Israel, including the newly imposed VAT tax that merchants were obliged to pay: a tax widely considered to be illegal under the international law governing occupations. "No taxation without representation," was the not-unfamiliar slogan of the day. Israel's crackdown was harsh: extended curfews on the town and army raids where soldiers confiscated cars and merchandise. There was widespread international support for the Beit Sahuris and vocal protests against Israel, including complaints from church officials and from Pope John Paul II. Beit Sahur, then and now a population of approximately twelve thousand, is approximately three-quarters Christian.

Beit Sahur means "the place of the night watch" and is the locus of Shepherds' Field—or Fields, as the Orthodox and Catholic churches have separate dominions. On Christmas

Eve 1989, with Beit Sahur in the midst of its peaceful rebellion, the message heard by shepherds watching over their flocks had a very special resonance: "Fear not for we bring you tidings of great joy" rang out, and Archbishop Desmond Tutu of South Africa emerged to address the crowd of thousands of Palestinians. Raja and I were among the throng, the only time, I must admit, that we had joined in the many religious celebrations that mark Christmas in Palestine. As an army helicopter hovered overhead, Tutu brought a message of hope for "peace in the land of peace" and voiced his support for "the struggle of Palestinian people to nationhood." Movingly, an Israeli peace activist, Veronica Cohen, also addressed the crowd: "I cannot wish you merry Christmas but I do wish you that this should be your last Christmas under occupation." Her wish seemed tantalizingly possible as Palestine's popular and largely peaceful rebellion against occupation garnered increasing international support. But alas, it was not to be.

Countless images of the Nativity place an ox and a donkey among the animals watching over the newborn babe in his manger in nearby Bethlehem, an ox—a castrated male cow—being presumably a better babysitter than his bullish counterpart. In 2012, stern Pope Benedict XVI threw cold water on this peaceful mammalian ensemble, pointing out that the Bible does not mention animals at the manger. At Shepherds' Field in 1988, however, I imagine Shomali's animated cows, led by Rivka, now a proud Beit Sahuri, joining their human companions in cheering Tutu's optimistic message.

"We deserve to have our freedom. We deserve to have cows," says one Beit Sahuri to Shomali. But he also admitted that Palestinians had no "cow culture," and so, in the midst of intifada turmoil, the community managed to send Salim, a university student, to the United States to learn to milk cows.

Reminiscing more than twenty years later, Salim said of his cows: "They are like human beings; some are kind and some are angry." The camera accompanies Jalal Qumsieh, the purchaser of the cows, as he returns for the first time to the shed where they were initially sheltered. He recalls how twenty people crowded in the shed to cheer the first birth of a calf: "It was like a miracle, like a baby from one of our families had been born."

The cows were not able to stay in their shed for long. After a posse of Israeli soldiers arrived and photographed the cows, an Israeli military order gave Beit Sahur twenty-four hours to shut down their farm. "We are dead meat," comments cow Ruth to Rivka. Jalal Qumsieh repeats the "exact words" of the military governor: "These cows are dangerous for the security of the state of Israel." The residents defended their cows despite harassment from Israel, including an eight-day curfew during which soldiers broke into their homes and overturned furniture and stored food in a search for the bovine criminals. But Beit Sahur's cow initiative could not survive the 1993 Declaration of Principles between the PLO and Israel (and the ensuing Oslo Accords), which brought an accompanying decline in collective resistance. "There is no need for Beit Sahur's cows. There is no need for the intifada," said one Beit Sahuri ruefully to Shomali.

As the film draws to a close, we see the remaining four cows in another rattling truck, being carted off for slaughter, a fate already met by the other fourteen of their cowpatriots: "We've been betrayed by both Israelis and Palestinians," Rivka observes. The older cows push Yara, a young white calf, off the truck: "Go Yara, run for it. Run for all of us." Tellingly, Beit Sahur's community activists also felt betrayed by their national leadership when the Palestine Liberation Organization signed

the agreements, which offered Palestinians only limited auton-
omy. "We dreamed of so much more," a Beit Sahuri woman
commented. But unlike Yara, they had no place to run.

During the Intifada, Beit Sahuris, like Palestinians elsewhere in the West Bank and Gaza, had sought Palestinian
domestic products to replace the ubiquitous Israeli goods that
dominated the market. With the establishment of the Palestinian Authority came a new economic environment, which
offered new opportunities amid some serious obstacles. Six
Palestinian dairy companies in the West Bank, most founded
as family firms in earlier times, began to develop new production lines and invest in modern equipment. Several new banks
opened, making loans to businesses available (the branches of
Israeli banks that operated for much of the occupation had
closed their doors during the Intifada). But there were heavy
restrictions as well. The Paris Economic Protocols that accompanied the Oslo Accords greatly limited Palestine's economic
freedom. The protocols mandated, for example, that Palestinians import Israeli products first in a number of fields, which
meant buying cows and feed from Israel, even if less expensive
options were available abroad. Still, for the first time, Palestinians began to operate modern industrial dairy farms in the
West Bank, albeit on a much smaller scale than their Israeli
neighbors.

Before the 1990s, cows were the lesser companions of the
large flocks of sheep and goats found in most farming and
herding communities in the West Bank, although small herds
of cows did exist. If we take a very long and very wide view on
the region in the past, cows and bulls were much more prominent. Cows in antiquity had both a practical and a sacred status in several civilizations in the Fertile Crescent, as well as
in ancient Egypt, where one of the most popular goddesses,

Hathor, was often depicted as a woman with a cow's head. Sacred bulls were worshipped throughout the region. Across the Mediterranean, gods in Greek mythologies had a pronounced tendency to transform themselves into bulls, most famously Zeus, who turned into a magnificent white bull to carry away Europa. And in the Sinai Desert, Moses came down from the mountain to find his people engaged in idol worship of the Golden Calf. He promptly ground the Calf into powder.

Today, the cow's majestic cousin, the water buffalo, is still a key working animal for Egyptian farmers along the Nile. Until the mid-twentieth century, herds of water buffalo, introduced to the region in the eighth century, also inhabited the wetlands of the Huleh Marsh in the Galilee. The Huleh wetlands, an area of more than 21,000 acres, was the home not only to the buffalo but to the greatest concentration of aquatic plants in the Middle East. It also served as a major site for migratory birds. The buffalo vanished, along with a number of other species, when the new state of Israel decided on a massive project to drain the marsh (called by the Jewish National Fund the Huleh Swamp) in the 1950s. The buffalos' human companions, Palestinian herders, mostly from the Ghawarneh tribe, had been forced to flee their homes several years earlier in 1948; some of their descendants remain in refugee camps in Lebanon today.

A rather melancholy-looking herd of water buffalo was reintroduced to Huleh's partially reflooded, although greatly reduced, waterscape in 1994, and they remain a minor tourist attraction of the Huleh Nature Reserve. But partial is an understatement; the small reflooded lake, as the nature reserve's website notes, is only a "tiny remnant" of Lake Huleh. The reserve constitutes only about 1 percent of the previous Huleh wetlands. Watching the Reserve's short film years ago after visiting a bleak display of Huleh's extinct animals, I was caught in the narrative's contradictions. The film praises the young state's engineering feat in draining the marshes, while simultaneously acknowledging some of the damage done to a precious ecosystem. As the toll of extinct animals flashes on the screen, the oddest note in the film is an uncomfortable claim that the marsh would have dried up in half a million years or so anyway.

Visiting Huleh this autumn, the feature film is now a 3-D celebration of migrating birds, although the viewer occasionally experiences the dangers they face as a shot echoes in the ear or smoke fills the theatre. Huleh's most recent achievement—stopping farmers near the reserve from using pesticides—is celebrated as coexistence. And indeed, there is cause for celebration: the lake and remaining wetlands are once again a resting place for migrating birds as they fly along the Great Rift Valley from Europe to Africa in the autumn and make the long journey back to Europe in the spring. We were fortunate one year to come to Huleh just when hundreds of rose-tinged pelicans rose from the water to the sky.

The draining of Huleh is a prime example of what Israeli environmentalist scholar Alon Tal calls Israel's "technological optimism," a major thread in the European founders' vision of Jewish settlement in Palestine, along with a strong dose of the Zionist ideology of redemption of the land. A nascent Israeli environmental movement in the 1950s made a strong, if ignored, case against the draining of the Huleh wetlands, arguing that the original reasons for the huge project were no longer valid: malaria had been eradicated and reclaimed agricultural land was available elsewhere and more cheaply. But, for the Jewish National Fund, the draining of "swamps" was axiomatically good, and Israel's most massive land reclamation project erased an ancient waterscape. It was a catastrophe for the animals of Huleh but also harmed, and continues to harm, humans. As Tal observes, the draining of the Huleh region removed an essential nutrient sink that had absorbed nitrogen and phosphorus, preventing their runoff into Lake Tiberias (Kinneret), one of the country's main water reservoirs. Israel is not alone in remolding the environment through technological optimism, and it is an increasingly urgent question whether such optimism is a cure for our environmental woes or a cause of the same. The example of Huleh suggests the latter. Consider, for example, India's relentless projects to build three hundred dams, despite the warnings of environmental scholars and the massive protests of local people.

Cattle were present in even more ancient Palestinian landscapes. Recently, Israeli archeologists uncovered the ten-thousand-year-old grave of a woman shaman in the Galilee: among the animal bones buried with her was the tailbone of a cow. Five hundred or so years previously, scientists suspect, the first herd of cows in the Near East was domesticated from the now-extinct wild ox or aurochs. For millennium after millennium, humans were more dependent on cows than on any other domesticated animal: cows were perhaps the oldest form of wealth. Cows and bulls were both worshipped and sacrificed in Bronze Age civilizations throughout the Mediterranean, as is evident in Homer's *Iliad*. (And they are still worshipped by the Hindu population in India, with twelve thousand cows roaming Delhi's streets today.) The giant, human-headed, winged bulls of Nineveh, Assyrian King Sennacherib's capital and now an archeological site in modern Iraq, are scattered in museums throughout the world, from Britain to Baghdad. But one giant winged bull, carved from a single slab about 2,700 years ago, continued to guard a Nineveh gate until it met a very contemporary fate: in the wake of the 2014 takeover of nearby Mosul by the Islamic State, a zealous adherent of ISIS blasted away its face with a drill. An Iraqi archeologist, Lamia Al-Gailani, told the BBC that she found it "the most iconic of what ISIS destroyed, going and boring the eyes of the Bull."

It is comforting to find intact less intimidating images of ancient cow companions. A cow head tops a clay lighting fixture from thirteenth century BCE, found in Megiddo in northern Israel. His face is comical, an ancient relative, I thought, of Amer Shomali's Rivka. Visiting the new Sebastia Archeological Museum in the Palestinian hilltop village of Sebastia, near Nablus, I spy several sarcophaguses, undated but of either Roman or Byzantine origin, adorned with paintings of cows. They reside in the courtyard of the shrine and Ottoman-era mosque of Nebi Yahya, dedicated to the Prophet John the Baptist, and one of the several putative locations of the prophet's severed head. Sebastia was a major or capital city of a succession of ancient kings, including Herod the Great and his son Herod Antipas, the latter, as the story goes, the somewhat reluctant beheader of John the Baptist at the demand of his stepdaughter Salome. In Sebastia today, the courtyard hosts both the mosque of Nebi Yahya (Prophet John) and the Christian Byzantine-era tomb of the same prophet, as well as a museum celebrating the many layers of Sebastia's history, offering us a more peaceful and inclusive message.

No cows are visible today in Sebastia, although families in the nearby village of Tell raise small herds of two or three cows per family. In the terrain of the central highlands, goats and sheep were both favored and favorable to the land's steep hills and deep wadis. Their milk products were also, it seems, more suitable to the digestion of the Palestinian Arabs who consumed them. A recent study by Jordanian scientists found that the majority of Arabs originating from the Mediterranean basin are intolerant to lactose—found in abundance in the milk of cows and less problematically so in goat milk. Interestingly, the same lactose intolerance is prevalent in Jews, with whom Arabs share a very close genetic heritage: in 2015, scientists at the Albert Einstein College of Medicine found that 75 percent of Jews were lactose intolerant. Thinking of uneasy Jewish and Arab stomachs, I wonder why, in our small land, two parallel dairy industries, a longstanding giant in Israel and a burgeoning one in Palestine, have made cows a binational obsession. Perhaps Thomas Hardy had it right in his novel, *Tess of the D'Urbervilles.* The master dairyman who welcomes Tess to work on her first day milking cows is askance when Tess drinks a little milk. "It had apparently never occurred to him that milk was good as a beverage," Hardy writes. The dairyman then exclaims, "Rot the stuff; it would lie in my innards like lead."

Prior to the coming of the Palestinian Authority, I usually only saw cows in the West Bank when we stopped alongside a favorite road to the Jordan Valley in springtime to enjoy the transient poppies growing next to a trickling stream that was doomed to disappear in the summer heat. Often, four or five scrawny cows and an equally thin shepherd boy also took advantage of this temporary water source. These were the baladi (indigenous) cows, adapted to heat, accustomed to a meager diet and little water. Across the Green Line in the Galilee region in particular, the scene was different. In 1880, European Jewish settlers founded the "first modern dairy," according to the Israeli Cattle Breeders' Association. At first they raised baladi cows, but several decades later, in 1921, Jewish farmers imported twenty-three cows and four bulls and began crossbreeding them with local cows to produce the hybridized Holstein Friesian breed that now dominates both the Israeli and Palestinian dairy industries. The long process of substituting goats and sheep with cows, so highly recommended by British agricultural officials, began with the introduction of European cow breeds.

Our skinny but hardy baladi cows bear little resemblance to these ponderous cows of Dutch origin. Today, baladi cows share the difficult conditions of their Bedouin companions along the same Jordan valley road, as more Bedouin communities are driven away from their previous grazing grounds in the Jerusalem wilderness. One such encampment sits beside a sign warning of unexploded land mines: near a clutch of Bedouin black tents stand a camel, a donkey, seven cows, and an assorted herd of sheep and goats. A hardscrabble existence, but perhaps better than the conditions of cows in the new dairy farms.

While Rivka and the other Beit Sahur cows are long gone, cow culture has clearly taken root in the development of modern Palestinian dairy companies in Hebron and Jenin. In a twist on the Beit Sahur story, the products of two of the major Palestinian dairies were among five products banned by the Israeli authorities in March 2016 from reaching one of the major markets—Palestinians living in East Jerusalem. Israeli restrictions on the Palestinian economy are not breaking news. The World Bank's quarterly and special reports have been documenting Palestinian economic decline for many years, and in 2016 the Bank was particularly alarmed by a "stubborn unemployment rate" of 27 percent (18 percent in the West Bank and a staggering 42 percent in Gaza). The bank was clear about the effect of Israel's control of the Palestinian economy: "Israeli restrictions . . . have pushed private investment levels to amongst the lowest in the world (in the Palestinian territory)," opining that if such investment was allowed in Area C, it could increase Palestinian GDP by 35 percent. A 2018 World Bank report had even more dire projections if the status quo of "long-lasting restrictions," particularly in Area C, continued: further economic deterioration exacerbating "economic and social fragility" and "fuelling renewed conflict and violence." When even small-scale projects supported by international donors to improve the lives of beleaguered Palestinian communities in Area C—such as solar panels or water facilities—are quashed by military order, large-scale investments there seem very remote indeed.

The new ban on Palestinian dairy products reaching Jerusalem was challenged. The Palestinian Authority retaliated with a boycott of five Israeli products, including those made by Tnuva. Collective resistance of a sort returned, if briefly, with the five affected Palestinian companies taking their empty trucks and demonstrating outside Ofer Prison. Cows continue, it seems, to be at the center of Palestinian/Israeli economic warfare. Throughout 2017, the Israeli ban remained officially in effect, but permission to bring products to Jerusalem was "granted" to Palestinian companies on a month by month basis, which seemed to me like an effective, if mean and short-sighted, way to exercise maximum control.

A visit to the leading Palestinian dairy enterprise—Al Juneidi and its modern factory in the southern West Bank town of Hebron—was in order. I asked Amal, assistant to the manager at Juneidi, if we could also visit one of the company's three dairy farms in the small village of Zeef, and she agreed. After the usual obstacles traveling from Ramallah to Hebron, Raja, Hani, and I turned into the factory gate and encountered Palestinian police escorting a cavalcade of cars, including, to our surprise, some Israeli military vehicles. Amal greeted us and was obviously wired: we had come on the heels of an unexpected meeting with the Israeli Civil Administration (staffed, just to note once again, by military officers) and Palestinian

Authority officials to discuss—and Amal hoped, attempt to solve—the problems of "the crossing" at Tarqumia, a checkpoint (now called a terminal) in the southern West Bank, where Juneidi trucks line up with products destined for Gaza.

The city of Hebron is about forty miles from Gaza. "We used to just drive to Gaza," Amal explained. "Now we must take products in sealed trucks, and Israeli officials at the Gaza crossing often make us take them out and put them on the ground—they are dairy products and shouldn't be in the hot sun." Almost a third of Juneidi's output goes to Gaza, which makes arrangements—or the lack of them—at the crossing into Israel and then into Gaza urgent matters. I recall when Gazan products were common in Ramallah markets, from soft drinks made at Gaza's 7Up factory, to bamboo furniture, to the limes that only Gaza produced and which came in spring, just in time for gin and tonics. But now traffic is only one-way, governed by an elaborate system of permits.

Amal, who obtained an MBA from Hebron Polytechnic, has been working for Juneidi for almost a decade, and most of the other employees in this administrative section are women, too, all head-scarfed and buzzing with enthusiasm. *Another important story of local industry*, I thought—employment opportunities for educated young women. Palestine, as in many other arenas, is an outlier in female labor force participation, which is unusually low, while female education is among the highest in the region. This is due to the fact that its major labor market since 1967 has been in Israel and pretty much limited to men working in construction. Female labor force participation has risen slowly since the 1990s (although female unemployment remains high) thanks both to public employment in the Palestinian Authority and to the development of companies like Juneidi, which today has more than five hundred employees.

Amal ushers us into the Juneidi meeting room, which is packed with displays—yoghurt, labneh (a cheese from strained yoghurt), long-life milk, buttermilk, and an array of salads. She offers us a glass of the fresh milk that has recently hit the Palestinian market; it is delicious. Raja, who is lactose intolerant, tries to make me drink his glass as well. To date, Juneidi has not been able to "export" its fresh milk to the East Jerusalem market, which consumes a substantial 14 percent share of its other products.

We are given brochures that feature two contented cows grazing on green grass: as dairies become more industrial, advertising, it seems, becomes more pastoral. Juneidi's three dairy farms are home to about four thousand cows; half of Juneidi's milk is purchased from independent farmers with smaller herds of fifty to a hundred cows. Today, all the cows are Holstein Friesian (nary a baladi cow in sight) and all, Amal acknowledges sadly, are bought in Israel. "We are a captive market," she says, "so Israeli sellers sometimes send us cows that are low in productivity or old." A month before, when I visited the chief vet at the Ministry of Agriculture, he also complained of this widespread practice. And it is not only cows that are sold in this captive market; everything from semen for breeding to vaccines for disease are also only made available courtesy of Israel. As we were visiting Juneidi, Gaza faced an outbreak of foot-and-mouth disease. Israel, with an elaborate list of what can and cannot enter Gaza, initially refused, according to Gazans, or delayed, in a charitable interpretation, the vital vaccine, finally allowing it in after a week of protest and negotiation.

On the drive to the Juneidi dairy farm at Zeef, we give a wide berth to the settlement complex at Kiryat Arba, located in yet another alphabetically designated area—H2—but one that is unique to Hebron. Under the 1997 Hebron agreement, Hebron was divided: H1 is Area A, controlled by the Palestinian Authority, and H2, according to the Temporary International Presence in Hebron (TIPF), "a mix of Area C and Area B." TIPF seems temporary no longer—the Hebron agreement was one more partial measure that was supposed to lead to a final status agreement in 1999, almost two decades ago. Today, Zeef is just outside the southern reach of H2, across Highway 60, which has also cut the town off from some of its lands. Further restrictions were placed on Zeef when the Israeli Civil Administration (here it is again) issued a master plan for the village in 2008 that further narrowed the village's boundaries. Whether it is any consolation that Zeef remained in Area A is somewhat doubtful, given the villagers' Bedouin origins and the loss of any grazing land.

Along the way, Abu Haitham, a manager at the factory, tells us how it all began at Juneidi with a young man riding an old-fashioned bicycle through the streets of Hebron, two cans of milk slung across the front. The bicycle is enshrined at the top of the gate at the factory. When two Juneidi brothers decided to form a company, established on May 20, 1982, it was during a period of "many risks and untimely surprises," as the Juneidi website aptly notes. Abu Haitham's descriptions of Juneidi trucks attempting deliveries to the northern West Bank during both the First and Second Intifadas attest that these risks and surprises continued.

The Juneidi dairy is entirely contained within Zeef village's narrow boundaries. It might seem strange to locate a dairy farm in this highly restricted Area A enclave, but Area A is the only secure territory for a Palestinian economic enterprise. When we turn into the farm's modest entrance, we find that it is in fact quite small, encompassing several sheds and a building for the twice-daily milking. The hills and valleys beyond are, inevitably, in Area C. There is thus no pasture, even if the protocols of modern dairy farming permitted cows to graze.

Abu Muhammed, the manager of the farm, greets us. He is lean and dark from the sun, clad in overalls and knee-high rubber boots. Raised in a Hebron-area village, he sought education: like many Palestinians, he seized every opportunity to advance himself, but his trajectory was often interrupted. He studied animal husbandry and veterinary medicine at an Egyptian university in the 1970s but his next opportunity for further training in these fields came almost twenty years later when development assistance came to Palestine after Oslo and he received a scholarship. He takes pride in the standards of health among the hundred or so cows under his care and in the hygienic conditions under which they give their milk for market.

"Would you like to see the calves?" he asks, leading us to a stall where a small calf is huddled next to a concrete wall. When I ask how long the calves stay with their mothers, Abu Muhammed answers "hardly a day." Even if a much smaller version of an industrial dairy farm, Zeef, it seems, has the practices of its much larger colleagues across the Green Line or in the Europe and the United States. In the United Kingdom, it is standard practice, for example, to remove a calf after thirty-six hours. Often, it is reported, the mother will bellow and scream for days.

He leads us first to the "dry" cows, who are in the period where they do not give milk. All are in pens under the tin-roofed shed, standing in muck, with a number stamped on them. It is hard to remember that cows in past times used to have names. These stationary cows are about three times as large as the baladi cows in the Jordan Valley. Although we can see green fields stretching beyond the cows, they are never left out to graze. Cows, like humans, must respect Area C.

Zero grazing of dairy cattle is not unique to Palestine (or Israel), although it is a practice that has come under increasing attack from a range of animal welfare organizations globally. I watch as the Zeef cows are funneled into the milking shed. Their udders are cleaned and attached to hoses. The milk begins to flow. Computers register production and all is hygienic, all is up to international standards. The cows stand still, hardly twitching their tails. We are a long way from the cows in Tess's nineteenth-century dairy who, Hardy notes, "show a fondness for a particular pair of hands." The only difference among cows that one can detect in the Zeef milking room is their level of production or their susceptibility to disease. "Mastitis can be a problem," Abu Muhammed admits. When cows are made to produce milk at a high yield, their swollen udders can lead to this agonizing infection. I look again at the cows at their milking stations. Can we be proud of a real Palestinian economic success against the many obstacles that Juneidi has faced? Can we afford to worry about the restricted and unhappy lives of these bovine animals who have nurtured our human journey for so long?

Abu Muhammed's pride pales in comparison to that of Prime Minister Benjamin Netanyahu (no mean hand at boasting) telling President Xi of China about Israel's "Super Cows." On a 2015 visit to China, he asked the head of the world's most populous nation (whose population is mostly lactose intolerant), "You know which cow produces more milk per cow than any other cow? You think it's a Dutch cow or a French one? No, it's a Jewish cow. It's a computerized cow. Every moo is computerized." And to give Netanyahu his due, Israeli cows (a better designation, I think, than the rather bizarre "Jewish cow") have the highest milk yield in the world. One Israeli dairy farmer told Bloomberg News that cutting-edge technology drives Israel's milk production—he scorns the traditional methods still sometimes used in Europe and asserts that cow farming belongs in the world of WhatsApp and Google. Cows have become virtual, rather than living, creatures.

Technological optimism indeed. But when the shiny machines and fast computers are weighed against the mechanized and confined lives of cows who are subject to them, it is time perhaps to hit the pause button. And the effects of our global cow mania are increasingly evident, as livestock density increases and alarming statistics circulate: 40 percent of all agricultural crops go to feed livestock, cattle contribute significantly to global warming through their methane emissions (the more down-to-earth terms are *burping* and *farting*), and livestock production may be the largest single driver of habitat loss. How then, to consider the fate of the melancholy cows in industrial dairy enterprises, whether a relatively small one like Juneidi or "Super Cow" dairies across the Green Line. Both, perhaps for different reasons, operate with policies of no grazing. These dairy cows have no exercise, shortened and solitary lives, and above all can never act naturally.

A debate rages at present on the virtues or vices of a return to grazing. Livestock grazing, or what is termed "holistic" grazing by Australian rancher Allan Savory, returns carbon to the soil and, he claims, can return the earth's atmosphere to something like preindustrial levels. Dangerous nonsense, replies environmental journalist George Monbiot, citing a daunting list of statistics that suggest carbon's upward trend is irreversible. I think the debate is important and that it should continue, but I must return to my small patch of land and the thirty-four thousand cows in Palestine (out of about 1.4 billion cattle worldwide) to ponder the question of how to balance human enterprise, and indeed Palestinian economic development under occupation, with animal welfare. Sometimes, in order to act, we have to think small.

I ponder computerized cows and our common lives. In museums, I have often passed quickly through the rooms devoted to a seemingly endless number of Dutch paintings featuring cows. But now I consider why Dutch painters of the seventeenth century were so fascinated with these animal companions. In the Tate Britain gallery in London, there is a luminous early-nineteenth-century painting by J.M.W. Turner, "Ploughing Up Turnips, near Slough," where men, women, and cows are partly engaged in mutual work and partly at rest together (one cow is eating the turnips), Windsor Castle in the background. The juxtaposition of the castle and the ragged laborers hint that we should not be nostalgic about the hard work of turnip lifting, but the closeness of human and animal also has a message. I think again of our contemporary cows, subject to constant rounds of artificial insemination and separated from their calves at birth, and I call to mind a different, more cheerful vision, from the poet Elizabeth Bishop. In her poem "Santarém," she recalls arriving, sometime in the 1960s, at a small port that sits at the intersection of two great rivers in Brazil, the Amazon and the Tapajos. Among "countless wobbling dugouts," she spies one in particular where "a cow stood up in one, quite calm/chewing her cud while being ferried,/ tipping, wobbling somewhere to get married."

"Where are we going, Rivka?" is not a bad question to ask ourselves as we think about our relation (or lack of the same) with one of our oldest human companions, now computerized and confined, like most of our world. Amer Shomali's film ends twenty years after the white calf Yara escapes into the desert wilderness below Beit Sahur. We see Shomali walking along a trail shrouded by steep cliffs. "Perhaps she is an old cow now," he muses. "Or perhaps she is dead and I am chasing ghosts." But he observes that sometimes to go on living, it is necessary to believe in something, and he decides to believe in a white cow living in a cave. In the last shot, Shomali enters one of the many caves carved into the desert cliffs. We hear a welcoming *moo*.

Wild pigs check out a Ramallah neighborhood at night.
(Credit: Bassam Almohor)

CHAPTER 6

A CONSPIRACY OF WILD BOARS

There is always a time, during our Friday morning hikes, when our walking group finds itself laboring up a hill, scrambling over boulders and brush, with the more sturdy and surefooted helping those like me, who have a tendency to slip and fall. When, one sunny spring morning in 2008, we reached the top, it was time for a rest. Saleh, a historian at Birzeit University and our walk leader, warned us to look under rocks for grouchy snakes, just waking up from hibernation. The Palestine viper, the only deadly poisonous snake in the country, can be particularly ill-tempered. Then we heard a noise from the brush, and something black, bristly, and big hurtled by, knocking my friend Samia down. It was a wild boar (*Sus scrofa*), probably a new mother protecting her young. Admittedly, her maternal sentiments are admirable and her social life praiseworthy: wild boars live in matriarchal groups of two or three reproducing females with their recent litters. Like their close relative the domestic pig (*Sus scrofa domesticus*), wild boars are smart, or what the scientists call "cognitively complex," with excellent spatial memories and navigation abilities. But, alas, wild boars are very large, often weighing in at about two hundred pounds, and their long snouts, tusks, and hairy visages are particularly unappealing and often frightening to humans.

Wild boars? I thought these hefty creatures preferred the Galilee. And aren't they supposed to favor forested areas near abundant water sources, as Mazin Qumsiyeh noted in his exhaustive *Mammals of the Holy Land*? Indeed, the only other time I had previously encountered them—at a fortunate distance—was in the tree-lined and water-rich Wadi Amud beneath the hilltop Galilee town of Safed. Wild boars evoked the huge hogs of my Midwestern childhood and reminded me of my physician father treating farmers wounded by the same: in one unfortunate incident, a farmer lost his hand. I have more-pleasant memories of a piglet my mother won at a raffle; the small pink pig appeared instead of the advertised ham, a good example of Midwestern small-town humor in the placid 1950s. My seven-year-old self enjoyed taking Piglet on walks until he mysteriously disappeared, perhaps to his fate as a ham. Wild boars, however, were another matter. Hearing a herd snuffling below us, I refused to descend any farther into the pleasant wadi.

But since Samia's tumble that day, increased sightings and distress calls from Palestinian farmers have signaled the wild boars' growing, some say skyrocketing, numbers in the West Bank. While that presence is not contested—a rare agreed-upon fact in the Palestinian–Israeli conflict—Palestinian farmers not only complain about wild boars destroying their crops but point an accusing finger at Israeli settlers.

Walking along Wadi Zarqa (the Blue Valley) near Ramallah one early July morning, Raja, Bassam, and I stopped in a patch of shade near where a farmer was tending a small orchard just above one of the springs that dot this beautiful wadi. In its western stretches, the wadi is also called Wadi Natuf, meaning "dripping" in Arabic and Hebrew. Whether blue or dripping, the stream along this wadi, in people's memory, always has had water. The northwestern face of Wadi Natuf has high limestone cliffs and caves, including Shuqba Cave where, in 1928, British archeologist Dorothy Garrod and a team of local Palestinian workers—all women—uncovered a stratified deposit from Mesolithic Palestine (12000–9500 BCE) including forty-five fragmentary human skeletons, flint tools, the remains of gazelles, and, interestingly, a partial skeleton of a domestic dog. Garrod named this culture of hunter-gatherers Natufian, deriving the name from the wadi of her discovery.

In 2013, the Palestinian delegation to UNESCO nominated Shuqba Cave as a World Heritage Site, citing Garrod's findings there and noting that Natufian culture represented "a critical point in the evolution of human culture in southwest Asia," when hunter-gatherers were in transition to agriculture and selectively domesticating both flora and fauna (remember the dog!). To date there has been no action on this submission. One hopes that the continued mining of rock and gravel at the nearby Natuf Quarry, in Palestinian territory but owned by an Israeli company, will not damage the cave before it can be protected. Two Israeli human rights organizations have filed petitions against the quarry for transporting natural resources across the Green Line, in defiance of both international and Israeli law. In an odd and unrecognized partnership, two nearby Israeli settlements have also protested, not on grounds of illegality, which they could hardly argue, but on the charge of nuisance and noise.

Back on the bank of Wadi Zarqa, the farmer, Abu Mahmoud, a sturdy man in his early fifties, has seen much to trouble him from his small patch of land deep within a valley. He remembers when he was a boy and the water in the stream was as high as his knees; now he says it is "just a fingernail," even in spring. Clearly, something in the "dripping" valley has changed. When we ask him what animals are nearby, he acknowledges, with some prodding from me, the gazelles who have inhabited this wadi at least since Natufian times. Gazelles, it seems, do not interest him. He is more concerned, even incensed, with newer incomers: wild boars. "Many of them," he tells us, and he assigns clear blame: "It's the settlers. I saw it with my own eyes. A truck pulled up on the road up there and dropped wild pigs with a winch. The truck said Tel Aviv."

Abu Mahmoud's direct friendly manner and seasoned air make him a convincing witness, but *really*, I thought, *settlers dropping boars with a winch*? Bronzed by the sun, Abu Mahmoud has a silver tongue: he obviously relishes telling stories, whether heard from others or from his own observations. I wonder if the pigs on winches could be a story taking flight from a shadowy image on a road quite high above his valley home. It makes more sense to me that someone, perhaps settlers, dumped a dead wild pig into the valley. The wadis of the West Bank have unfortunately become dumping grounds for much more than one or two dead animals.

When Abu Mahmoud goes on to say that he heard that settlers had also released a *nimr* (leopard) who died shortly afterward, my doubts increase. Arabian leopards inhabited Palestine for millennia, but sightings drastically decreased in the early twentieth century, and now we can only hope that perhaps somewhere in the Naqab (Negev) Desert or in the wadis above the Dead Sea a leopard or two might survive. However, I am sure that Abu Mahmoud is right about several things, particularly the increase in the wild boar population and the sad diminishment of water in this beautiful wadi and its surrounding springs. By all evidence, Israeli settlements *have* diverted water from many nearby springs, several of which are now off-limits to Palestinians. A few miles away in Nabi Saleh, a Palestinian village of about six hundred people, residents marched every Friday for six years toward the village spring, Ein Al-Qaws, which had been taken over by settlers from nearby Halamish. The villagers suspended the demonstrations in 2016, after suffering more than three hundred injuries and several deaths from Israeli army tear gas and rubber bullets; protests have continued sporadically since then. Most recently, on December 15, 2017, in a slap heard round the world, teenager Ahed Tamimi, who had just learned that her fifteen-year-old cousin Mohammed had been shot in the head, struck a soldier during a protest. In its wake, Ahed, her mother, and other relatives were detained. Ahed was sentenced to serve eight months in prison.

The spring remains off-limits to the village. A necessity for both farmers and animals, springs are also one of the great pleasures for a weary walker in the West Bank's karstic limestone landscape. But they are now sites of bitter human conflict.

The reports of settlers instigating wild pig invasions of Palestinian land are not just from lone farmers like Abu Mahmoud. In 2012, the mayor of Deir Istiya, a farming village of some three thousand people in the Salfit district of the West Bank, told CNN that settlers had to date released about three hundred pigs into Deir Istiya's orchards and fields. Deir Istiya is surrounded by nine Israeli settlements, and the remarks of the mayor came in the wake of a well-documented settler attack, where graffiti was scrawled on the village mosque and three cars were burned. Such direct settler intervention into the lives of Deir Istiya is confirmed and well publicized, but the release of wild pigs seemed to me more murky. Both Jews and Muslims abhor pigs as unclean, refusing to eat them and, I thought, not so eager to handle them as well. And other forms of human intervention in the environment, whether walls, wastewater, or increases in human settlement and human garbage, seemed obvious factors. On the outskirts of congested Ramallah, the omnivorous wild boar can now be spotted near the garbage heaps of new high-rise housing projects, while other wildlife has fled. The Separation Wall also brings wild boars closer to Palestinian towns and villages, notes Imad Atrash of the Palestine Wildlife Society. What is beyond doubt is that the wild boar population in Palestine has soared, and many communities are suffering from infestations of this large mammal with outstanding survival skills.

Globally, wild boars are a truly invasive species—perhaps not to the degree to which humans upset the environments *they* inhabit—and they appear in increasingly unusual places. Sites of various boar invasions in Germany, for example, include a hairdressing salon, a cinema, and Berlin's Tegel Airport. At least, however, in Germany and other European countries, revenge may be taken and boars consumed. A friend tells me that at her United Nations agency, the Palestinians shudder when the topic of wild boars comes up, while the Italian head of the agency salivates.

Pigs, whether large or small, could be considered invasive to the entire Eastern Mediterranean, including Palestine, if we consider a very long stretch of time. A genetic analysis of recently found three-thousand-year-old pig remains on Israel's Mediterranean coast indicated that the pig came from Greece. The speculative scenario is that pigs sailed with the Philistines—the people of the sea—around 3,200 years ago, mixing with, and then coming to dominate, the local boar population. The origin of the seafaring Philistines, who founded settlements along the southern coastal region of Canaan from

Gaza to Ashdod in the late Bronze Age, is not entirely known, although Palestine has inherited their name. In his history of the Mediterranean Sea, Cambridge University historian David Abulafia affirms that the Philistines came from somewhere in the Greek world, and, more grandly, that they were "the kinsmen of Agamemnon and Odysseus."

Thinking about pigs and these Greek heroes—an irresistible coupling—I recall that when Odysseus finally returned home to Ithaca, disguised as an elderly pauper, his old nurse recognized him by a scar a wild boar had inflicted on his leg. And even more to the point, when Odysseus and his men landed on the island kingdom of the beautiful if minor goddess Circe (Kirke), Circe promptly gave the first search party a drug-laced drink, struck each man with her rod, turned them into swine, and drove them into her pig pen. As the *Odyssey* recounts: "they took on the form of pigs—swinish heads, grunts, and bristles— only their minds stayed as they had been. So they were penned there, weeping in the sties: and to eat Kirke threw down for them acorns mast and cornel-berries." With a combination of good advice from Hermes, plus what seems to have been an excellent sexual performance with Circe, clever Odysseus managed to persuade Circe to return them to human form. Thinking of pigs arriving on our shores from Greece, I wonder if one or two sailors remained in porcine form.

Myths of men and pigs have circulated in the Near East for a very long time: Adonis, beloved of Aphrodite, was killed by a wild boar in the forests above Byblos, in northern Lebanon. Versions of his death and resurrection have circulated throughout the region: in Canaan, where his name was derived (from *adon*, the Canaanite word for lord) and among the peoples of ancient Mesopotamia and Egypt, where his resurrection myth is related to Osiris. The wild boar who killed Adonis, sent on his mission by a jealous Artemis, remained nameless as far as I can determine.

Pigs feature in another sacred tale some centuries later, when Jesus was on his sojourn around the Sea of Galilee. On its eastern shore, according to several accounts in the Gospels, he met a man (or two men) possessed by demons. The demons pled with Jesus: if you are driving us out of this man, let us go into the herd of swine. The demon-possessed herd then stampeded into the lake and drowned. At the site today, which maintains its old Arab name of Kursi, are the ruins of one of the largest Byzantine monastic complexes in the country. A huge boulder is enshrined on the hill above, presumably the designated site of the miracle. The church, like many structures around the lake and down the Jordan Valley, was destroyed in the earthquake of 749 CE, but human hands have restored quite a bit, and the mosaic floor with its geometric patterns and medallions of flora and fauna is quite astonishing. Mosaic figs, pomegranates, grapes, geese, cormorants, and many kinds of fish abound, the animals more damaged by time and human hands than the plants. Indeed, we live in a land of ruins and remains, stories and silences, devastation and fragments of the past.

In our present difficult environment, I continue to wonder about Palestinian convictions of direct settler violence, and the fears that fuel these suspicions. I have speculated that families in southern West Bank villages, unprotected by police, have a greatly enlarged fear of attacks by the shy, and relatively rare, hyena. Farmers in the northern West Bank suffer real damage from wild boars, who are in abundance. They also experience many forms of settler violence, and so it seems natural to attribute a wild boar infestation to the settlers. Structural violence, what Teju Cole terms "cold violence," and intentional physical "hot" violence are a potent mix that is hard to separate.

In the early years of the new millennium, I spent some time talking to Palestinian women in Amari refugee camp near Ramallah. It was a time of harsh Israeli reprisals during the Second Palestinian Intifada, as well as what was all too aptly called "security chaos" on the Palestinian side, where militias, or simply young men with guns, were on the streets and the Palestinian police largely ceased to function. Time after time, women and girls told me not of the very real fears and insecurities they experienced in the camp, but instead of worries over tales of Palestinian moral dissolution and corruption, usually located in the cafés of nearby Ramallah, places of "dancing and drinking," where young middle-class men and women, with their more globalized lifestyle, act, in the eyes of these young women in a nearby refugee camp, inappropriately. A café called Stones—the only word in our conversations in English—figured prominently. Fear and insecurity are shapeshifters: immediate threats to life and security transmute into forms of moral panic.

Wild boars are not in their bulky selves particularly adept shapeshifters, but the stories around them are. And if there is a modern-day Circe casting spells on our pig population, farmers and officials in the town of Salfit and the surrounding Salfit district would point their fingers at settlers. Salfit is a large agricultural town west of Nablus, surrounded by Israeli settlements, including the mega–settlement complex of Ariel to the west, which began in 1977 with two Israeli army tents pitched on a hill, followed in August 1978 by forty Israeli families. Ariel now hosts at least twenty thousand Israeli settlers. Below hilltop Ariel, the town of Salfit has long been a hub for neighboring villages. Now, under the Palestinian Authority, it is the district seat. In April 2014, Palestinian farmers in the Salfit district appealed to all Palestinian and international bodies to help protect their dwindling crops: "We have encountered heavy losses in our wheat and barley crops, where the pigs destroyed them completely." The appeal was the culmination of a series of reports of the crop devastation caused by wild boars. But what are the causes of this major pig infestation?

As in Deir Istiya, previous documented experience of settlers destroying crops and disrupting olive harvests in the Salfit district give added purchase to a belief that settlers are behind the infestation. But again, is it true? And if so, can it be proved? The well-respected Applied Research Institute–Jerusalem (ARIJ) noted in 2009 that the Wall is a major factor in the increase in the wild boar population, pushing the animals to search for new habitats. The Israeli human rights organization B'Tselem, writing earlier in 2007, attributes the boom to raw sewage runoff from the massive settlement complex of Ariel polluting water sources near Salfit and killing off other wildlife while drawing wild pigs to its delicious detritus.

Salfit seemed to be at the center of this particular storm. So, I inveigled Raja into yet another mission, this time to explore both sewage and wild boars in a visit to the beleaguered town. When I explained our twin goals to a café-loving colleague in Ramallah, she had a vinegary comment: "Well you are really living on the edge!" I fear she had a point: we are going to investigate, to put it crudely, "rivers of shit," as the rock group the Fugs sang in a 1969 hit (well a hit for some of us at least), and also one of the world's less appealing mammals fond of the same. Not that such excremental rivers are unique to Salfit: looking down from the magnificent view at the Mar Saba desert monastery below Bethlehem, the unwary walker can be tempted to descend to a shining silver ribbon of water in the a nearby wadi only to find, by using his or her nose, untreated sewage from Jerusalem.

Edgy or not, we departed Ramallah with our friend and taxi driver Hani. We drove north toward Nablus on a dusty Sunday, at the height of the spring khamsin, the yellow wind that comes blowing from the Sahara Desert in May and dries out the green of plants and the hearts of humans. A sign announced a turn west to the Israeli settlement of Ariel; we squinted to see a small notice to our destination, Salfit. Israel has given the four-lane road going west toward the coast the grand name of the Trans-Samaria Highway, and Ariel itself was declared the "capital of Samaria" by Prime Minister Benjamin Netanyahu during a tree-planting visit there in 2010. According to the Hebrew Bible, Samaria was the capital of the ancient Kingdom of Israel; the resonance and the reversion are telling.

Slowly the realization dawned on me that I had not been to the fertile valley that cradles Salfit for almost thirty years, although our annual supply of some of the best olive oil in Palestine comes from there, courtesy of a colleague of Raja's brother. In the years of the First Intifada, Salfit was famous for more than its excellent produce: it was a center of civil resistance against the occupation. Memories of my fateful last visit in 1988 had been buried in the flood of events that followed that tumultuous peak year of the First Intifada. In March 1988, I traveled to Salfit in a rusty bus, accompanying a group of academics from the United States and Europe. A long-planned Birzeit University conference on "Twenty Years of Occupation" had finally happened, in the relatively secure space of Jerusalem's Ambassador Hotel; the University itself was closed by military order. At the time, our conference committee thought that the occupation years were drawing to a close and sought to chart Palestine's independent future. We were not alone in that belief: six months later, the Palestinian National Council, meeting in Algiers and buoyed by the mass uprising in the Occupied Territories, would proclaim an independent Palestinian state committed to the principles of the Universal Declaration of Human Rights. But it was not to be.

In the bus, I chatted with Professor Herbert Kelman, a scholar and practitioner of conflict resolution from Harvard University, and his kindly wife Rose (with a bag of cookies on her lap), as we made our way down a narrow winding road toward Salfit. The Trans-Samaria Highway was still in the future. Beshara Doumani, a young historian at Birzeit who now heads the Center for Middle Eastern Studies at Brown University, negotiated with young Palestinian men at a series of barricades. They removed the stones for our bus and then patiently put them back. Salfit was a "liberated village," and the young men, the *shebab*, were determined to defend it. In the town center, Beshara had begun to speak to a young activist he knew when the cry came: "Army, army," from the village rooftops. As Beshara wrote at the time: "Within seconds, the town square became hauntingly empty."

When our bus was stopped on the way out of town, Beshara had to negotiate not with the *shebab* this time but with the Israeli army. Explaining that we were a bus from Birzeit University with visiting foreign academics, we were finally permitted to continue after a half an hour of questioning. Sadly, a delegation of five of us returned a few days later to Salfit with a letter from all the bus passengers. We were paying a condolence call: the army had killed two young men, saying that soldiers were rescuing a hijacked "tourist bus." Fake news is not just a twenty-first-century phenomenon.

Three decades later, we are met by another barricade: a barred entrance to Ariel, the once small settlement redesignated as a city after it passed the population mark of twenty thousand, the benchmark for cities under Israeli municipal law. Conveniently for them, Israeli settlers and settlements operate under Israeli law, while Palestinians in the West Bank are ruled under military law. We bypass Ariel's imposing entrance; the road continues to Salfit through an open gate. But roads in occupied Palestine have weary histories. Israeli soldiers erected that barrier in 2000 and firmly shut the gate to Salfit for over a decade. Residents had to take a long and winding road around Ariel to reach home. In 2012 the entrance was finally opened for Palestinian ambulances and public transport, and a year ago it became accessible for all.

A closed road is a powerful symbol for the problems faced by the twelve thousand residents of Salfit and the seventy thousand Palestinian residents of the Salfit district, comprising the town of Salfit and eighteen villages. When we arrive at the municipal office of Salfit's water engineer, Saleh Afaneh, a sturdy man in a crisply ironed shirt, he seats us at a desk loaded with stacks of proposals, all stamped with variations of "Sewage Treatment Master Plan." These are plans Saleh and his team have been working on since 1996, just after the coming of the Palestinian Authority, and continue with today, two decades later. The dates on the plans range from last month to twenty years ago. It turns out the Fugs' lyrics are more relevant than I imagined:

> I've been swimming
> In this river of shit
> More than 20 years
> And I'm getting tired of it

Whatever fatigue he has experienced over the years is not evident in Saleh's determination to put forward Salfit's case once again, if only to three local residents with little or no power to alter the situation. His opening comment is bold: "I say Salfit is the biggest problem for Palestine," he declares. Bowing briefly to Palestinian public opinion and the national, religious, and global consensus on the centrality of Jerusalem, he backtracked only slightly. "Okay, Jerusalem is the biggest problem, but we are number two."

His reasoning and his series of PowerPoint maps are persuasive. "In the Salfit district, Israeli settlers now outnumber Palestinians," Saleh tells us. I am still capable of being shocked. Yes, Israel controls more land than Palestinians in what is called, rather sadly, the "remaining" West Bank, but Palestinians number well over two million, while Israeli settlers are only about one-quarter of that, at half a million. (Both figures exclude East Jerusalem.) Salfit and its neighboring villages, however, have the misfortune of being on the western slopes near the Green Line, and crucially, almost on top of the precious Mountain or Western Aquifer, a major water source for both Israelis and Palestinians. No respecter of a green line drawn on a map in 1949, the aquifer lies under both sides of this human division, although the bulk of its recharge area (about 70 percent) lies in the West Bank. The proportions of water allotted to the two parties in the Oslo Accords are almost the reverse, with Israel given 80 percent of the reserves.

Ariel's rapid growth has much to do with its strategic location near this aquifer. And Ariel keeps on growing. Aside from its more than twenty thousand residents, Ariel also hosts about ten thousand students at its Ariel University Center, formerly the College of Judea and Samaria. The university's establishment was clearly illegal under international law, human rights activists say once again wearily, as was that of Ariel itself. In his tree-planting moment, Prime Minster Netanyahu declared Ariel an "indisputable" part of Israel. Along with the Gush Etzion settlement bloc near Bethlehem and the Maale Adumim bloc near Jerusalem, the Israeli government has pledged to retain Ariel in any negotiated settlement. It is a pledge sealed in concrete: the Wall includes a separate circular loop around Ariel (sometimes called the Ariel Finger), cutting deep into West Bank territory. When former Prime Minister Ariel Sharon made public his plan in 2003 to build the Ariel loop as part of the Separation Wall, there was a flurry of international protest, including from the Bush administration: the *Los Angeles Times* reported that "For weeks, the White House has warned Israel not to loop the main fence around Ariel, for fear that the line would harden into a de facto political boundary that would render the forming of a contiguous Palestinian state difficult." A flurry of words versus a steady pouring of concrete: the Ariel loop now cuts about twenty miles into the West Bank.

And the concrete keeps pouring: the Wall, part completed, part under construction, and part planned, is due to circle around the other settlements in the Salfit district, as well. Completed, the Wall would cut the Salfit district into three parts. "There would be no more Salfit district," Saleh concludes, pointing to yet another melancholy map.

Our discussion is joined by the new mayor of Salfit, elected only a few days before in Palestine's long-postponed municipal elections; the municipality's environmental expert also draws up a chair as do several staff members. Thanking a young man who serves us an anonymous sweet carbonated beverage, I hope we deserve the generous attention paid to us and ask my usual question: What about wild pigs? "Wild pigs are a big problem," the mayor says, and voluble Saleh extrapolates:

"People—especially women and children—living on the outskirts of the town are afraid to leave their homes at night." "Hundreds and hundreds of wild pigs," an assistant to the mayor adds vehemently. The mild-mannered environmental expert notes that he has visited several people in Salfit's hospital who have sustained injuries from encounters with these massive creatures.

Saleh shows us a slide of three young boars lying dead beside Ein Al-Matwi, the most powerful of the town's two nearby springs. They look more like my Midwestern piglet than the hairy beasts of my imagination. These young pigs have been poisoned, and, confirming my view of porcine intelligence, Saleh explains that wild pigs avoid any site when poison has been put down after the first deaths. One warning seems to be enough: Rhineland forester Peter Wohlleben observed that when hunting horns sound for the first time each year in the forest, wild boars swim across the Rhône river to Geneva, where hunting is outlawed.

Interestingly, the unpublished memoirs of a Ukrainian physician and avid hunter who arrived in Palestine in 1930 describe a hunting expedition at Ein Al-Matwi that undercuts the view that wild boars are twenty-first-century newcomers to the Salfit District. Sometime before World War II, Dr. Rodenko and three Palestinian hunters arrived at the spring to shoot partridges. Rodenko took aim at a bird but was startled by a loud noise and missed. A huge wild boar appeared. Rodenko followed the boar and shot him in the spine. A donkey was summoned. It took six men to lift the boar onto the dragooned donkey, who "staggered like a drunk man." One of the hunters was Muslim and couldn't eat pork, so Rodenko gave him three partridges instead.

Rodenko's gun is long silent; the doctor, who settled in

Ramallah after serving in Gaza during the early years of the British Mandate, died in the 1960s. At least since 1967, no other Palestinian hunter of wild boars has emerged. To date, Israel has not given Palestinians, including security personnel, permission to shoot boars in Areas B and C, despite repeated requests. Villagers in Tell, an agricultural community along the Trans-Samaria Highway, have been asking the Israeli authorities for permission to use buckshot, showing proof of the devastation of their crops caused by the pigs, but to no avail. Wild boars are much less likely to be found in the narrow urban enclaves of Area A, where Palestinian police are able to use firearms, although they have their urban moments.

I ask the question of the hour: Are settlers releasing the wild pigs? Saleh's answer is measured: "At first," he says, "but not now." The quiet environmental expert looks skeptical and shakes his head; I suspect that he may not be a believer in this form of settler direct action. A man who had not spoken before expresses the more widespread popular view: "Of course, the settlers release them," and he adds for emphasis, "they also release dangerous snakes." Everyone's opinion, whether expert or not, is received with attention. It is quite true that the high walls of Ariel protect the settlers living there from wild pig incursions, and I can certainly imagine one of Ariel's armed guards frightening boars away from Ariel and into the valley toward Salfit. But the most important danger released from Ariel remains its untreated sewage flows that foster wild pig infestation.

Saleh stolidly shows us a series of slides of sewage pollution, both from Ariel and from the industrial waste of the hilltop Barkan industrial zone, an Israeli enterprise on Palestinian territory. As well as wild pigs, the sheep, goats, and cows raised by Salfitis and nearby villagers drink from these polluted streams and graze on plants whose source is sewage. "I don't buy milk or meat from the villages anymore," says Saleh sadly. "I know what might be in it." And then he shows a picture of kids swimming in a polluted spring in Wadi Qana. Our environmental expert adds that he has even found fecal matter in the small spring that is inside the town of Salfit. Another slide shows dumped solid waste, presumably from Ariel, on Palestinian land. Saleh is nothing if not fair in his accusations: "Unfortunately sometimes Palestinians bring it in their trucks from Ariel for money."

I, too, have walked down a hill to a glittering stream in one of the wadis around Ramallah only to be hit with that telltale smell. Sometimes the hilltop settlements that surround northern Ramallah are clearly responsible, because one can see the beginnings of the streams trickling down from these locales. But Palestinians, whether without any other recourse or simply for convenience, do not always safeguard the health of their springs and wadis. Before our Ramallah neighborhood was connected with a new sewage system—a very happy moment—we used to call Abu Khaled and his truck to empty our cesspool. We had built it deep and with strong concrete walls to prevent seepage to the groundwater, but we never followed Abu Khaled to see the destination of our particular contribution.

The stacks of plans in Saleh's office attest to his and his team's determination over the past two decades to establish a sewage treatment plant for Salfit. After their first proposal was refused by Israel, Saleh's team began working with a German government–funded development organization. The logical place for the plan was near the Ein Al-Matwi spring, where Rodenko once hunted. Ein Al-Matwi is located in a wide agricultural valley where the plant's treated wastewater could be used to irrigate fields. But Ein Al-Matwi, like more than half of the Salfit district, is in Area C, and the Israel Water Authority once again rejected the plan. Salfitis are stubborn and not fond of giving up: letters were sent to everyone in the Palestinian Authority, from President Yasser Arafat on down, seeking help. In 2002, Salfit engineers were forced to accept another location in a more distant and very narrow wadi where it would be too expensive to pipe and pump treated water. Afaneh told us that the German partners are standing in the way, asking the question "Why treat Salfit sewage when it will merge with the untreated sewage from Ariel only five kilometers away?"

The question is apt; even though plans for a new Ariel sewage treatment plan included a 2016 start date, no such plant is currently in operation. But the problems go even deeper. German hydrologist Clemens Messerschmid has lived and worked in the Palestinian territory for about two decades. In 2016, he summed up the serial water crises faced by Palestinians as "induced scarcity." "The West Bank is blessed with a treasure of groundwater," Clemens commented, but he continued, "this is also its curse." Since the onset of the occupation in 1967 and for half a century afterward, Israel has forbidden Palestinians from drilling any new wells that utilize the Western Aquifer or its adjacent springs. Tellingly, this remains true today even though Israel, with its successful desalination initiatives along the coast, is now a major exporter of water.

Both present and past Israeli governments seem determined that Ariel and its long finger into the West Bank can never be reversed. Even in more halcyon days of Israeli–Palestinian negotiations for a final peace settlement, Israeli officials would not budge on Ariel and proposed discussing a land swap instead. "They say we can swap for land near Gaza," says Saleh with a tone that indicates Palestinians have been offered a piece of moon rock. The first slide in Saleh's presentation is left on the screen as we sip our strong coffee. It reads, in capital letters, "DANGERS." Today, Salfit is enclosed, while boars roam freely. The town cannot expand into the 50 percent of Salfit district that is Area C, so residents are forced to build new housing on some of Salfit's precious agricultural land. "We are killing ourselves," Saleh says emphatically.

We drive back on a twisting road that takes us west of Salfit. When we turn onto the highway, we see the extensive Barkan industrial zone on a hill on the northern side of the road. Another Israeli project, Top Greenhouses, graces the opposite hill. Cows are grazing on the grassy strip that traces the flow of Barkan's chemical waste, and several other cows are drinking from the polluted stream below. Several black goats are also grazing on the hill. The bright green line down the hill from the Barkan industrial area is the last verdant spot we see as we drive home. The gray-green olive trees in village fields have a coating of dust, and the land beneath them is already cracked. Israel's hilltop settlements, enclosed in walls, may well have sprinkler-fed green lawns, but the thought is less than comforting. I try a more consoling thought: annual rainfall in Jerusalem and Ramallah is usually higher than London, and Salfit even higher. True enough, but we are back to the curse of abundant groundwater that is under another's control and planned for another's purpose.

As we turn at the Tappuah junction, with its multiple checkpoints, we see a sign pointing to a new unit of Israel's Civil Administration: Environmental Protection, Samaria. As with other parts of the Civil Administration, the unit is staffed with army officers. The unit's slick website has a strong focus on a favorite topic: sewage. The unit pledges to stop the "illicit transfer of waste to Judea and Samaria" and notes cooperation with the Palestinian Authority, as well as new sewage treatment projects in both a settlement and a Palestinian village. Coming from Salfit, it is easy to be cynical. Geographer Shaul Cohen, who also heads a peace studies program at the University of Oregon, has written that environmental voices in both Israel and Palestine are measured against a "matrix of nationalism." While acknowledging that Israelis and Palestinians are in "very different places of power and statehood," he asserts that environmentalism for both can be an "unaffordable luxury."

But environmental reform for Palestinians may equate to survival. Given our increasingly fragile ecosystem, environmental cooperation on water is an urgent concern, but, like the end of the half century of Israeli occupation, it sometimes seems unreachable. The fate of the Israeli–Palestinian Joint Water Committee established in the Oslo Accords is sadly instructive. At the time, the committee, with both the Palestinian and Israeli sides wielding a veto, was supposed to approve new water projects, including the proposed Salfit plant, as well as protect (and share) water resources. But, as far as I can determine, the Israeli side insisted that it would veto Palestinian projects unless projects in Israeli settlements were approved. And thus it went on, until a new head on the Palestinian side balked at approving settlement initiatives, and the Committee collapsed. On January 15, 2017, the Palestinian Authority and Israel signed an agreement to renew joint work, whereby Israel should sell thirty-three million cubic meters of desalinated water from the Red Sea annually to the Palestinian Authority. Given that Israel has about one hundred desalination projects, this could be a feasible project, but even so, it is hard to see how it addresses the rights of Palestinians to the groundwater under their feet. And, almost a year later, the new Joint Water Committee, according to the head of the

Palestinian Environmental Agency, has never held a meeting. Meanwhile, however, the stubborn persistence of the Salfitis has had a measure of success: in July 2018, Saleh Afaneh told me that, finally, their waste water treatment plant would go ahead. But, he added, Salfit would begin the project "before the Israeli even think to solve their pollution." And, he noted in capital letters, the problem of wild boars is "WORSE AND WORSE DAY BY DAY."

As Clemens Messerschmid observes, Israel's Military Orders 92 and 158, issued in the first year of the occupation in 1967, are still in force and require Israeli permits for almost every Palestinian activity regarding water, including drilling, repairing wells, installing pipes, creating irrigation pools, harvesting cisterns, and on and on. Any "joint" committee working in this legal framework will be unable to operate fairly. But as I look again out the car window at the cracked earth, I think that there is water underneath. Our porous limestone landscape is friendly to humans, animals, and plants. "In Praise of Limestone," a favorite poem of mine by W. H. Auden, evokes the springs "that spurt out everywhere with a chuckle" in such a landscape. The poet writes that when he imagines a "faultless love," what he hears is "the murmur of underground streams/ what I see is a limestone landscape."

We, Palestinians and Israelis, inhabit this friendly landscape, but it is hard to hear the murmur of water and its promise. But it is also essential if we are to both fairly share the aquifer now as well as preserve it for the future. More than a century ago, the war-weary Siegfried Sassoon called Palestine his Arcadia. It was only the "deeds of men" that he scorned, in a brief but evocative 1918 poem that he wrote during his Palestinian sojourn:

On the rock-strewn hills I heard
The anger of guns that shook
Echoes along the glen.
In my heart was the song of a bird,
And the sorrowless tale of the brook,
And scorn for the deeds of men.

In Sassoon's Arcadia, humans are the invasive species and alas, remain so today, outstripping any invasion of wild boars. The dramatic increase in the population of boars is real, as is damage to Palestinian crops and fields, but to solve it, our hills and valleys must no longer be sewage and garbage dumps. In those beautiful valleys, we, too, hear the echoes of guns, of soldiers and settlers, rather than the murmur of underground springs. Walking along a Ramallah wadi below the ring of settlements that sprang up after the signing of the Oslo Accords, John Viste, both an avid bird watcher and the former head of an agency promoting Palestinian education, commented: "Our only hope is geologic time." Too long a stretch for desperate Palestinian farmers, shrinking gazelle populations, and escalating boar invasions, as well as for Saleh in Salfit, still determined to improve his town's lot. But the environmental imagination needed to understand our precious limestone landscape, found more in poets than planners and politicians, is something to cherish.

Jackals on the move. An illustration from a review of
"Where the Jackals Howl." *(Credit: Photoillustration* Tablet magazine;
original photos Shutterstock. Reproduced with permission)

CHAPTER 7

THE HOWL OF THE JACKAL

I click on YouTube and listen to recordings of jackals howling as night falls on Jerusalem. Their howls are both eerie and entrancing. One of the Arabic names for a jackal—*wawi*—is clearly inspired by this creature's unique sound, somewhere between a cri de coeur and a cackle. The hills that surround Jerusalem have long been favorite haunts of jackals, but these jackals sound their cry from a small urban nature reserve inside the city—Gazelle Valley, near the West Jerusalem neighborhood of Givat Mordechai. Residents there had fought to preserve the valley, the home of a small herd of gazelles, and found themselves neighbors as well to some very vocal jackals.

On the other side of the city, Ali, a resident of the Mount of Olives, tells me he often hears jackals howling from the wadis below his hilltop home. He also notes that prime jackal territory is around one of the massive Israeli settlement blocs in Arab Jerusalem, Pisgat Ze'ev, which is sprawled on the eastern slopes of Jerusalem's much-expanded municipal boundary that cuts into the Jerusalem wilderness. Pisgat Ze'ev, with more than fifty thousand residents, is the largest of the ring of Israeli settlements established after 1967 around East Jerusalem, and jackals have clearly benefitted from the concomitant increase in the delicacies of human garbage.

When our neighbors built their house in the early 1980s, our Tireh neighborhood was on the far outskirts of Ramallah. Their kin, comfortingly, told the couple that they were moving to live with the jackals. Walking in the hills near Ramallah, I only encountered a jackal once. At sunset several decades ago, I was ascending a stony slope; it was emerging from behind a thorny bush. We were both scared out of whatever wits we possessed and parted hastily. It was silent; I was the one who let out something like a howl. Today, new urban neighborhoods stretch far beyond our house in Tireh, and I have not heard the call of the jackal in the Ramallah night. My friend down the street, Carol Khoury, tells me this is simply because I don't stay up late enough. A keen bird watcher and a night owl herself, Carol's powers of observation are formidable. In the late evenings, she has seen jackals padding along near her house. "Perhaps you saw wild dogs," I interject. "Jackals," Carol replies politely but firmly. Jackals do seem to be moving closer to our town. When Abu Mahmoud, the farmer in Wadi Zarqa near Ramallah, listed the animals he observed around him, he ended with jackals. "They are new," he said, pointing to a rubber irrigation pipe that a thirsty jackal had chewed through. "We never had them before." Jackals are equal-opportunity raiders: Israeli farmers also complain about damage to their irrigation pipes from jackals stealing a drink.

Unlike the diminishing number of hyenas, this other, much smaller, carnivore is flourishing on both sides of the Green Line. When an "ecological bridge" was built over a highway in the Galilee, the Israeli nature enthusiasts who had lobbied for it hoped it would aid the circulation of the diminishing gazelle population. Instead, it has become a favorite conduit for jackals, foxes, and wild boars. In 2016, Israel Nature and Parks Authority experts told *Haaretz* newspaper that they still hoped the shy gazelle would finally make her way across the bustling road. The Israeli army has made several openings in the Separation Wall for small animals, but the iron logic of security dictates that they must not accommodate a person, however thin. I suspect that the flexible jackal may be able to squirm through them.

Environmental activists have gone to Israel's High Court for injunctions to change the course of the Wall, citing threats to key cultural and physical landscapes and the devastating effects of ecological fragmentation on wildlife. One partial victory was the 2015 order freezing construction of the Wall through the village of Battir, a UNESCO World Heritage Site for its 2500-year-old olive terraces and aqueducts. But the Wall continues its way through the southern West Bank, blocking ecological corridors for threatened mammals like gazelles and ibexes. Through it all, jackals manage to adapt and thrive.

Jackals are also passionate about the food and carcasses that can be found in the country's many landfills, and "infestations" of jackals have been reported, particularly in the hills around Jerusalem, in the Golan Heights (where the cattle pens of Israeli settlements are a jackal favorite), and on the coast between Haifa and Tel Aviv. In the last few years, the Israel Nature and Parks Authority has been killing more than a thousand jackals annually in an attempt to control the population, but to no avail. In the earlier years of the Israeli state, a massive poisoning campaign targeting jackals apparently did cause a decline in population.

Neither campaign had the duration or scope of the extermination assaults on the jackal's distant cousin in North America, the coyote, in the late nineteenth and early twentieth century, but the lessons from this campaign are instructive. Dan Flores, in his book *Coyote America*, writes that between 1883 and 1928, the state government in Montana, urged on by sheep ranchers, paid bounties for 886,367 dead coyotes, consuming two-thirds of the entire state budget. Similar campaigns waged against wolves resulted in a substantial decline in their numbers, but coyotes "remained undiminished despite the extraordinary number reported killed." Today, coyotes are found in the eastern United States as well, with one famous young male coyote found loping through New York City's Central Park in 1999. Coyotes are highly adaptive, social or solitary as conditions dictate, and clearly quite able to relocate. Jackals share some of these traits, which perhaps we should learn to value as we are buffeted by, and must adapt to, global warming and extraordinary climate "events."

An excess of jackals—at least as defined by humans—is nothing new in historic Palestine. Writing for the Palestine Exploration Fund in 1866, Henry Tristram reported that the jackal "swarms in incredible numbers in every part of the country." The golden jackal (*Canis aureus*), sometimes called the Asiatic or common jackal, lives throughout North Africa and the Middle East. During the British Mandate, these numerous jackals substituted for absent foxes when a nostalgic British police officer founded a club to hunt them, near the Palestinian town of Ramle. Historian Michael Cohen (quoted by *Haaretz* journalist David Green) described the scene: Jackals "were chased on horseback across cactus-strewn fields; members could buy especially tailored red coats with the insigna 'Ramle Vale Jackal Hounds.'"

No bigger than a medium-sized dog, the jackal, with a distinctive strip along the back and a dark tail, is one of the world's least fussy eaters, munching on carrion, small animals, insects, plants and fruit (jackal diets are about 50 percent vegetarian), and the odiferous offerings of our garbage. Not for nothing is the jackal termed "nature's cleaner."

In his trip to Palestine in the 1940s, naturalist Victor Howells described the "lesser jackal," as he calls the golden jackal, as a nuisance, killing chickens, goat kids, and lambs and descending in large packs from the hills to "devour corn, eat watermelons, pumpkins and even grapes in the vine-yard." Recently, I visited Abu Suleiman in the village of Ramoun, on the eastern slopes below Ramallah. We sat outside his small stone house under a fig tree. Abu Suleiman's sheep were in a pen a few yards away, and I asked him if wild animals threatened his herd. "No," he said, "but jackals eat the chickens."

The jackal might put in a claim as the most ubiquitous of mammals in the land between the Jordan River and the Mediterranean Sea, although there are more varieties of bats (there are eighteen bat species among the fifty-eight identified mammal species found in Palestine/Israel). Jackals could also be cited for their marital devotion, usually mating for life. Their sense of smell is extraordinary as well, about one hundred times more sensitive than that of humans, and their night vision is excellent. It is, however, unlikely that these outstanding jackal traits will convince the Israeli Nature and Parks Authority to replace its logo of the elegant and noble-looking ibex, at present an endangered animal, with the survivalist jackal, who has glided through the history and stories of both Palestine and Israel.

In Arabic poetry, including Palestinian verse, the graceful gazelle is the animal most cited by a long shot. Although pre-Islamic verse does have a number of odes to camels, gazelles feature in even more ancient verse from the region: "My beloved is like a gazelle," sings the Song of Solomon. The jackal, with his coarse hair and unearthly shriek, is clearly no poetic substitute. But in fables, satirical tales, and more recently in fiction, jackals abound as narrators and tricksters. In the twentieth century, the jackal also emerged as a troubled and allegorical figure in the Palestine–Israel conflict.

When Raja was a student at the Quaker-run Friends School in Ramallah in the 1960s, the Arabic curriculum still included a small slice of one of the region's most enduring cycle of stories. This was not *One Thousand and One Nights*, the series of tales told by graceful Scheherazade to ward off her execution, but stories narrated in a large part by two jackals, who gave their names, Kalila and Dimna, to the ancient collection. Thirty years later, when my nephew Aziz was in the same school, Kalila and Dimna had vanished. And indeed, the disappearance of this great classic, which originated somewhere in India as *The Fables of Bidpai*, or even earlier with the Buddha's Birth Tales, is a story in itself. As the writer Doris Lessing noted, one could claim that this "ocean of tales" has traveled more widely than the Bible, with twenty translations in English alone before 1888.

Kalila and Dimna was translated into Persian in the sixth century and into Arabic several centuries later in the Abbasid Period, which witnessed a flowering of Arabic literature and of translations into Arabic of Greek, Persian, and Syriac literary and scientific classics at the great library in Baghdad, the House of Wisdom. Each translator of *Kalila and Dimna* has added a twist—or in the case of the most famous Arabic translator in the eighth century, Ibn al-Muqaffa, a few moral precepts that he felt were missing. With its lucid and succinct style, al-Muqaffa's text is considered one of the first masterpieces of Arabic prose. Al-Muqaffa had a point in adding a dose of morality: the tales within tales within tales that constitute the cycle are not particularly high-minded. The book does commence with an air of instruction, when the wise Professor Bidpai attempts to educate the rather nasty and incompetent King Dabschelin on the arts of kingship. However, the professor quickly turns over his role as narrator to the jackal brothers. Kalila is intent on the downfall of a peaceful bull who has been adopted by the lion king. The noble lion permits vegetarian beasts designated as members of his kingdom not to be devoured by him or his kin. Kalila plots to convince the lion that the bull is fomenting a coup and deserves to be killed and eaten, while Dimna tries to restrain Kalila's envy and malicious ill will. But as Kalila tells a tale to Dimna, which reminds Dimna of another, which reminds Kalila of an even better one, the jackals' narrations are more instructive in how to avoid being a victim of power than in curtailing the exercise of the same. A number of commentators thus compare the "lessons" of Kalila and Dimna to Machiavelli's *The Prince*, with its emphasis on how to exercise cold-blooded power effectively.

Machiavellian jackals recall the stories Native Americans tell of the trickster coyote, although this distant relative of the jackal has a more elevated sacred status. As the coyote "goes along" in Native American tales, he manages to create the whole of the North American continent, molding the mud into plains and mountains and creating humans, an act he might later regret. These first Americans saw Coyote as a deity, but the European settlers who came later viewed him as a pest that must be eradicated. The coyote and jackal are figured in the human imagination as both friends and enemies: they resemble each other even more in our tales than in their physical characteristics. Jackals and coyotes evolved separately, the coyote from a wolf ancestor who stayed in North America and the jackal from one who traveled across the land bridge to Asia and evolved as she moved across the region. In ancient Egypt, people deemed this small mammal a god and companion to humans, as Native Americans did cousin Coyote on the faraway American plains. Anubis, the jackal-headed god, embalmed the bodies, guided the souls, and guarded the tombs of the dead.

In our contemporary period, the jackal has not entirely lost his ability to narrate and has certainly retained his howl. Two haunting stories, one from the beginning of the twentieth century, by Franz Kafka, writing in German in Prague, and one a half century later by Amos Oz, writing in Hebrew in Israel, represent the jackal as a powerful, if ambiguous, character who figures—more explicitly in Oz and more mysteriously in Kafka—in the conflict between Arab natives and European settlers in Palestine.

"Where the Jackals Howl" is the title story of Amos Oz's 1966 short story collection. Jackals move in and around these uneasy, often tense, stories of life on an Israeli kibbutz somewhere in the Galilee in the years before the 1967 war. The unnamed narrator describes how the kibbutz searchlights, mounted on the perimeter of the barbed wire fence, blur the nighttime surroundings so that "we cannot see the jackals as they spring out from their hiding places." But when a young jackal cub is captured in a trap, older jackals emerge from the gray light and surround the wounded animal: "Jackals, huge, emaciated, filthy and swollen-bellied. Some with running sores, others stinking of putrid carrion."

Small mammals grow huge and threatening in Oz's story, and then another horrifying transmutation takes place. A troubled and troubling character, Mattiyahu, who has just seduced his daughter, summons a dream. He recounts a vision where "herds of thin dark people" stream down the hills, "racing over the ruins of deserted villages." They uproot the fertile valley, pillage homesteads, and climb over walls "like demented apes." Then, Mattiyahu addresses an unexplained figure, perhaps the reader, perhaps his daughter, or maybe himself: "Suddenly you too are surrounded, besieged, paralyzed with fear. You see their eyes ablaze with primeval hatred, mouths hanging open, teeth yellow and rotten, curved daggers gleaming in their hands." Thin dark men racing over ruined villages can hardly have any connotation but Palestinian Arabs whose villages, now ruins, once dotted the Galilee landscape where the kibbutz sits. Neither Oz the writer nor the youthful narrator, an Oz stand-in, are synonymous with Mattiyahu and his nightmarish (and racist) vision. But in Oz's fictional landscape, Arabs and jackals are clearly intertwined: both are menacing, both besiege the lighted safety of the kibbutz, and both stink of decay. The writer himself is haunted by both man and animal in these stories that clearly emerge from Oz's life experience.

Oz, born in Jerusalem to immigrant parents, moved to the kibbutz of Hulda in the Lower Galilee in 1955 when he was only fourteen, two years after his mother, Fania, committed suicide. In rebellion against his right-wing father's politics and sedentary life of scholarship, the young teen joined the socialist-inspired collective life of the kibbutz and changed his name from Klausner to Oz, Hebrew for strength. In his revealing memoir, *Tales of Love and Darkness*, Oz finds that just changing his name doesn't make him the man he wants to be. He contrasts himself with the other young people in the kibbutz: "Those boys were magnificent stags, and I was a miserable worm. The girls were graceful gazelles and I was a stray jackal howling behind the fence." A powerful image that carries over into his fiction: Oz, excluded, weak, and solitary, is a howling jackal.

The kibbutz, despite or because of its collective life, is a lonely and strange place for Oz and compels him to write, and in fact to write about jackals. He writes in his memoir: "It is night outside and jackals are howling hungrily very close to the perimeter fence, I will put them in the story too." And so he does. He also imagines his mother's reaction upon first arriving in Palestine from the cosmopolitan city of Prague: "How did my young mother respond to the sand dunes . . . the rocky hillsides . . . strings of camels carrying building sands . . . the dark blue nights punctuated by howls of jackals and echoes of distant gunfire?"

Camels and jackals, as well as the stony landscape they inhabit, are indeed alien creatures in the European landscape of meadows, cottages, and goose-girls evoked in Oz's mother's tales of "a genuine, cozy, world, far away from the dusty tin roofs, the urban wasteland of scrap iron and thistles, the parched hillsides of our Jerusalem . . . It was enough for me to whisper to myself 'meadow' and at once I could hear the lowering of cows with little bells tied around their necks, and the burbling of brooks." The jackal's howl offers no such reassurance. The kibbutz, in Oz's fictional imagination, is besieged both by the "thin dark men, " the dispossessed Palestinians who race over their ruined villages, and by their jackal equivalents, also outsiders, who stink of death. The story creates a symbolic link between Arabs and jackals, but the relationship is more complicated than that, as befits a haunted Israeli writer.

Jackals (and Arabs) are not only outside threats to the inhabitants of the kibbutz; they also live in their hearts and haunt their imaginations. An everlasting curse, Oz writes, "stands between house dwellers and those who live in the mountains and ravines. It happens sometimes in the middle of the night that a plump house-dog hears the voice of his accursed brother. It is not from the dark fields that this voice comes; the dog's detested foe dwells in his own heart." The very terrain of Palestine, with its mountains and ravines, looms over the lighted safe space of the house or kibbutz. But the enemy also dwells within us, Oz seems to be saying: he is an "accursed brother." The curse that stands between the domestic and the wild, the dog and the jackal, the Jew and the Arab, cannot, in Oz's fiction, be lifted.

Domestic dog and wild jackal merge in the terrifying opening scene of Ari Folman's 2008 animated film *Waltz with Bashir.* Enormous slavering doglike jackals or jackal-like dogs, larger than either, pound through the streets of Tel Aviv, knocking over the city's ubiquitous café tables. Their eyes shine. When the narrator wakes from this nightmare, he goes on a quest to remember a waking horror—the 1982 Israeli invasion of Lebanon that he, a soldier then, has blocked from his mind. The nightmare jackals are both the dogs of war and, as one critic suggests, the living dead, the cadavers of all those killed in that terrible war, which ended in the massacre of Palestinian civilians in Sabra and Shatila by troops of the Lebanese Phalangist militias, aided by the searchlights of the Israeli army. Like Oz's dark men, the jackals are a reminder of past crime.

Franz Kafka took a different approach to Arabs and the jackals they live alongside: opposing them, rather than conflating them. "Jackals and Arabs," a particularly eerie Kafka story, may, in my reading, be set in context of the encounter in Palestine of a European settler and a Palestinian Arab native, as well as in the multiple realms of Kafka's imagination. With a Kafka tale, every interpretation is a minefield. Philosopher and cultural critic Theodor Adorno wisely remarked of Kafka's stories: "Each sentence says 'interpret me,' and none will permit it."

This strange "animal story," as Kafka insisted on calling it, firmly rejecting the term *parable*, was published in October

1917 in a monthly review, *Der Jude* (*The Jew*), edited by Martin Buber, later the first president of Hebrew University in Jerusalem. "Jackals and Arabs" was recommended to Buber by Kafka's friend Max Brod as one of the most "Jewish documents of our time," an interesting remark, as Jews have no direct presence in the narrative. And Kafka was the opposite of a joiner; he remarked in his diary, "What do I have in common with Jews? I have hardly anything in common with myself." Nonetheless, he was close to the liberal Jewish circle in Prague that organized talks by Jewish thinkers, such as Buber and Ahad Ha'am, and discussed subjects ranging from Zionism to Hassidic folk tales. I pause and think about Prague, the home city of Kafka, as well as Amos Oz's troubled mother. It is tempting to place her, beset by the howl of jackals and distant gunfire, beside the European narrator of Kafka's tale as he arrives at an unnamed place populated by Arabs and jackals.

In Kafka's brief tale, a European traveler arrives at an oasis, where he is unable to sleep because of a distant howl from a jackal. Suddenly, however, what was once far away is quite near. "Jackals were swarming around me, eyes gleaming dull gold and vanishing again," he says. But these jackals, unlike those who gather in Oz's tale, speak. They tell the narrator that they have been waiting for him "back to the first mother of all jackals," waiting for someone from the "far north" to rid the jackals of Arabs. The narrator finds himself pinned down by two young jackals who had locked their teeth in his coat and shirt. A pair of sewing scissors "covered with ancient rust" is produced, and the narrator is implored to draw blood from the Arabs and end this "very old quarrel" that divided the world and restore the land to "cleanliness, nothing but cleanliness," where every beast dies a natural death with no meddling from Arabs. But the Arab caravan leader comes, cracking his great whip, and explains that every European is offered the rusty scissors by the jackals. His entourage produces a camel carcass to throw to the eager jackals. The narrator observes: "They had forgotten the Arabs, forgotten their hatred, the all-obliterating presence of the stinking carrion bewitched them."

Historian Jens Hanssen, in a long essay on "Kafka and the Arabs," finds himself bewildered by the "reluctance of most Kafka scholars to acknowledge that 'Jackals and Arabs' is about the question of Palestine." As befits a historian, he situates the story in Kafka's own attitudes toward Zionism, colonialism, and Jewish identity, while also examining the reception of Kafka in the Arab world.

Whatever else the animals in Kafka's stories are, I read them also as real animals from a writer who is both interested in other species and obsessed and horrified by cruelty. After Kafka became a vegetarian, he visited Berlin and stood looking at the fish in the Berlin aquarium. "Now I can look at you calmly," Kafka remarked, "I do not eat you anymore." In the other story accepted by Buber at the same time as "Jackals and Arabs," entitled "A Report to the Academy," a "former" ape delivers a report of his brutal capture, maltreatment, and attempts to transform himself into a human to escape his torments.

I also read the jackals, the European narrator, and the Arabs of the caravan as creatures of Kafka's imaginary Palestine, a site that was on his mind for a number of years. The sewing scissors encrusted with rust offered to the narrator and other European travelers before him is a striking image of an absurd and useless weapon, encrusted with the rust of ages, offering no escape from the burden of the past. However, it is the last line of Kafka's parable that haunts me: The Arab leader is breaking camp and says that they will leave the jackals to their business. Then he adds: "Marvelous creatures, aren't they? And how they hate us." This sentence echoes in my mind with one change: "Marvelous creatures, aren't they? And how we hate them."

Jackals today are perhaps more ignored or disdained than hated. The virulent extermination campaigns against the coyote in the United States are certainly not equivalent to the Israeli Nature and Park Authority's more mild cull of jackals. But in a world that is increasingly dominated and shaped by human activity—our anthropocene era, heralding, some say, the "end of nature"—jackals and other adaptable animals will live ever closer to us, seeking opportunities to thrive through our garbage, our gardens, our fields, and the nooks and crannies of our cities and towns. To be sure, the golden jackal may be under threat in some locales: jackals were declared endangered in Greece in 2003, largely due to habitat loss from the intensification of agriculture and human superstition (we could call it hatred), resulting in widespread use of poison bait. Although a campaign by the World Wildlife Fund and Greek environmentalists seeks to aid jackal survival, wildfires sweeping Greece complete the triad of dangers. In response to pressures here, our golden jackal—that amazingly adaptable survivalist— has been moving out of the Middle East and into southern Europe in large numbers and has even been found in northern Germany and Switzerland, although I wonder if the tidy Swiss leave enough garbage to satisfy the small scavenger.

Are jackals, then, invading Europe? Many environmentalists view invasive species as a threat to native animals and plants and work (and dream) for a restoration of a "natural" or native habitat populated by the fauna and flora that belong there. Biologist Chris Thomas proposes a more dynamic view.

Acknowledging that we are in a period of mass extinction, he brings into focus animals and plants that adapt, survive, and evolve in our quickly changing environments, arguing that "if we are prepared to accept biological gains as much as we regret losses, we can take a much more optimistic view of conservation." He does not minimize the escalating species losses, but finds biodiversity flourishing on a globe where "human glue" has "brought together previously isolated biological worlds into one 'virtual continent.'" From the repopulation of Europe by jackals, wolves, bears, wolverines, and lynx to the Asian harlequin ladybirds in his own backyard in Yorkshire, Thomas finds new biological riches. His view is controversial, given the devastating decline of many species with at least one-quarter of mammalian species threatened with extinction. However, it is certainly consonant with the movement of jackals.

The expansion of the golden jackal across Europe is not a comeback, like the reintroduction of wolves or bears, which inhabited European forests for millennia until their near extermination. Northern Europe is new territory for the jackal, whose range had been from northern Africa to the Indian subcontinent, including parts of southeastern Europe but not Europe's western or northern reaches. The golden jackal has now been spotted in thirty European countries, posing a legal dilemma to scholars and a question of life or death to the jackal. Is the jackal an alien species, and thus possibly subject to eradication campaigns, or should it be a protected species? Legal scholar Arie Trouwborst of Tilburg University in Norway, working with biologists from Slovenia, argues that the jackal should be a native protected species under international law. Only species introduced by humans can be considered alien species. The jackal has come to northern Europe entirely on its own.

I would not be able to weigh the gains of the jackal over the possible losses in Palestine of the gazelle or the ibex from habitat loss and human hunting, explored in the next chapter. There is no such scale; those losses would be irretrievable. But I can hope that we can see jackals as "marvelous creatures" that we no longer hate but live beside in a common world. Jackals, like camels, came over the land bridge from North America more than ten thousand years ago, finding home and habitat in the Middle East, as well as other locales along the North Africa–India axis. Our own species, *Homo sapiens* (whether we deserve the name of not), migrated out of Africa to the Middle East perhaps a hundred thousand years ago. We are all migrants.

In his mythical form, the coyote in North America created the world as he went along and molded humans to inhabit it. In our region, the jackal-headed god Anubis eased our passage to death. The doors to human life and death are opened by these carnivore cousins. Marvelous creatures indeed, and how we live beside them.

CHAPTER 8

STILL WILD: GAZELLES, IBEXES, AND WOLVES

At last, a gazelle. On a winter walk down Wadi Qelt, a deep gorge that stretches from below Jerusalem to Jericho, Gerard Horton, taking a day off from his many duties at Military Court Watch, pointed to the steep hill opposite our path. A gazelle picked her way up a stony slope. It had been far too long since I had seen this daintiest of creatures in the hills and now, the day of the inauguration of Donald Trump as the 45th President of the United States, I cherished this heart-lifting encounter.

This was also a rare morning when I did not click obsessively through the websites of the Israeli and Palestinian presses, a malady I suffer in common with a sizeable part of the population, and whereby we are constantly "updated" on the daily flow on unnerving incidents and equally unnerving rhetorical flourishes from politicians. But I also managed to miss the news one day in September 2015. I was traveling and full of other obsessions: Are we sure we have enough time to get to the airport (checkpoints!) and emerge unscathed after the lengthy security procedures? Raja remarked wearily that we should have left the day before.

In the throes of travel anxiety, I missed a crucial environ-

Mountain gazelle in southern West Bank.
(Credit: Imad Atrash)

mental report that day. More than a year later, when I returned from Wadi Qelt that January day and, in a spirit of equality, googled both *Palestine gazelle* and *Israel gazelle*, the bad news surfaced on my screen. My mood plummeted. The International Union for Conservation of Nature (IUCN) had reclassified the "Israeli gazelle" from vulnerable to endangered. The Union's evaluation followed the release of figures showing the gazelle population in Israel declining by 70 percent in the last fifteen years: from ten thousand, according to Israel's Nature and Park Authority, to an estimated two thousand, adding the qualification that one thousand "additional gazelles" may be living in areas where they are "not counted."

Not counted! Could these be gazelles living with us in our patchwork Palestinian Authority? The mountain gazelle (*Gazella gazella*) is perhaps the most iconic wild creature in the Holy Land. Slender and elegant, this diminutive relative of the antelope is a figure of grace in texts from the Bible to contemporary Palestinian and Israeli poetry. Over centuries, even millennia, her range has extended from the Galilee to the Dead Sea, with perhaps a special preference for the hills of Jerusalem and the central highlands. In the 1980s, on late afternoon walks in the Ramallah hills, Raja and I often spotted a gazelle, sometimes accompanied by a yearling, threading her way among the stone terraces and the gray-green olive trees. Startled, she would leap, her white underbelly flashing. Sometimes several other gazelles we had not noticed would follow her lead. Although experts give the color of her coat as reddish-brown, she looked gray-brown to me, almost the color of the olive trees under which she wandered, perhaps because her hair is smoky at the tip. She was, in other words, lovely. Once, ascending a hill to the village of Deir Ballut, I came upon a fawn, tied loosely by a house, in the eerie quiet of

Palestinian villages during the First Intifada. The wide-eyed look of most mammalian young was amplified in her slender face, still without horns. A pet or food in hard times, I didn't dare to ask.

Today, the contending human habitations around Ramallah leave little room for the native gazelles. A new ring of Israeli settlements has arisen on the surrounding hilltops since the signing of the Oslo Accords in 1993, and Palestinian cities, particularly my city of Ramallah, have experienced a building boom on the restricted portion of West Bank land allotted to them. Palestinian housing project after housing project marches down the hills near Ramallah, accompanied by mountains of rubble from their construction. Gazelles are rarely spotted, but a fortunate walker who gets away from the city environs or the confines of Israeli settlement may meet this delicate animal before it bounds away once again.

A recent pocket guide to mammals in the Middle East by Chris and Tilde Stuart notes that the populations of the mountain gazelle in Yemen and western Saudi Arabia, once some of their main haunts, have been greatly reduced by hunting. The largest remaining populations, the authors say, are in Oman, Israel, and Palestine. Reading this, I didn't know whether to cheer because gazelles are still with us or to mourn their loss elsewhere in the region and worry that our small patch of land between the Mediterranean and the Jordan is a poor last refuge. Whether a recent Hebrew University study is correct in identifying some genetic differences between our mountain gazelle and the Arabian mountain gazelle, making ours a unique species, seems to me to matter less than preserving the remaining animals, whatever their genetic quirks. And mountain gazelles in our Palestinian corner are indeed under threat.

Gazelles have been hunted for food in Palestine and the

rest of the Eastern Mediterranean since the Stone Age. For the six centuries of their rule, hunting was a favorite pastime of Ottoman sultans, a royal art displaying the sultan's equestrian abilities in the pursuit of leopards, gazelles, and other large game, including on occasion lions and tigers. As historian Alan Mikhail points out, European monarchs, Ottoman sultans, and Mogul emperors exchanged gifts of exotic animals, either for royal menageries or for imperial hunts. Commoners were not allowed to hunt in the large areas reserved for the sultan. But the widespread introduction of firearms to the Middle East in the late nineteenth century (beyond their use by the Ottoman Army) and the decline and fall of the Ottomans changed the terms of the encounter between hunter and hunted. In their Galilee and Syrian habitats, roe deer and Syrian bears became extinct during the first half of the twentieth century. The former, a denizen of the wooded hills, was perhaps equally a victim of deforestation as of hunting. Encouragingly, roe deer have been reintroduced to one nature reserve in Jordan. There was also a lone sighting of a Syrian bear and cub in Lebanon's Bekaa Valley in 2016.

Along with roe deer, several species of gazelles throughout the region suffered significant reversals in the twentieth century, compounded by the century's endemic war and conflict. In Palestine, hunting during both World Wars was responsible for a major decline in the population of mountain gazelles. Today, they are endangered by loss of habitat, but also, I came to understand, once again by hunting. Because I have never come across a hunter while walking in Palestine, I had not realized the dire consequences of the renewal, and indeed escalation, of Palestinian hunting in the post-Oslo years until I had many discussions with wildlife activists.

Hunting, particularly of gazelles and birds, is embedded in

long-standing Palestinian traditions. Before 1967, my friend Rita's father, Abu George, a pharmacist in Bethlehem, frequently went out in his prized Jeep for a day of hunting with his pals and his hunting dog Mina. He usually brought back game birds, which the family grilled over charcoal. Rita also remembers her childish distaste for the sour meat of a gazelle on at least one occasion, adding the Arabic word for rotten. Rita, like all the children of Abu George, was taught how to shoot. When the Israeli army ordered Palestinians to turn in their guns after 1967, Abu George, like many others, hid his rifles in a well. After 1995, some were eager to pick up the guns of their fathers again. Perhaps the only virtue of the pre-Oslo period of direct Israeli military occupation, when Palestinians were forbidden weapons, was a sharp decrease in hunting in the occupied territories.

Across the Jordan River, the mountain gazelle, some say, is nearly extinct. Erosion of habitat is a major cause, but so are the Jordanians, who like Palestinians have a long hunting tradition. (Indeed, about 70 percent of the Jordanian population is of Palestinian origin, with the remainder often having Bedouin roots.) Jordan has legal restrictions on hunting: guns must be specifically licensed for the hunting of gazelles or boars, automatic weapons or artificial light cannot be used. But it is possible to evade these strictures in the Jordanian wilderness, where a new danger to gazelles has arisen: the advent of the avid and wealthy hunters of the Gulf. In January 2016, a dozen lifeless gazelles were sprawled on the car hoods of cheerful hunters as their convoy of cars, some with Qatari license plates, crossed the border from Jordan to Syria. And yet, the Jordan Tourist Board continues to promise visitors a chance for "marveling at herds of gazelles and oryx and migrating birds." It is true that twenty Arabian oryx, a bulky, desert-loving antelope with strikingly long horns, were reintroduced in Jordan's Wadi Rum, fortunately a protected area, in 2007. Herds of gazelles, however, are a memory from the recent past. At present, the country invokes this memory to manipulate tourists, but, I hope, the herds could return, thanks to a new generation of Jordanian environmental activists.

In the 1990s, I often heard firing in the wadi below our house interrupting the quiet of a Friday morning, most people's day off. *Training*, I thought. *The new Palestinian security services are training. Training* was the watchword of that decade, whether "democracy" training, a favorite activity supported by the international community, or security service training, also an arena of massive donor funding. Midway through that decade, just as the headquarters of the Palestinian Authority was established in Ramallah, I encountered a peculiar form of training when Raja and I were fired on by an overexcited group of young men who spied us walking in a valley on the outskirts of Ramallah. They thought, it seems, that either we were Israeli settlers or, much more likely, an illicit Palestinian couple that deserved a warning. The latter might have been flattering for a decidedly middle-aged husband and wife if the bullets that struck a nearby stone were not alarmingly close. I still think (I hope) that these guys were just trying to scare us. When Raja and I made it (shakily for me) up the hill to a Palestinian post, we complained to the officer who replied, tellingly, "But the *shebab* (young men) like to shoot, they are training." The intent was more malevolent the only other time a gun was fired directly at me. One day in 1989, during the First Palestinian Intifada, I was standing on our lighted glass balcony. At that time, Israeli settlers still drove through Ramallah, guided by a yellow line that the Israeli army had painted in the center of our street. A passing Israeli settler, probably going home to the nearby Dolev settlement, fired at me, shattering the window and my nerves. Although I emerged in one piece, I have an inkling of what it is like to be trapped in a deadly spotlight as hunters (even when forbidden) use car beams or other high-powered lights to hold a gazelle in their sights.

Rat-a-tat-tat disrupted Friday morning quiet well into the 1990s. But don't the security guys have a day off on Friday, too? Talking to those more attuned than myself, I found that they were indeed celebrating a day off—by taking their new guns into the hills to hunt. "The hunting was most intense in the hills north of Ramallah, near Birzeit," Imad Atrash said. That made sense; the police and security personnel were concentrated in the Ramallah area where the new Palestinian Authority had its headquarters. Ordinary Palestinians, steeped in a legacy of hunting, also took up guns, whether legally or illegally. In the chaos of the early 2000s, they may well have been joined by other armed men, driven by poverty as well as the pleasure of the hunt.

Most of this hunting is illegal, as most guns held by Palestinian civilians remain unlicensed. Strictures on hunting, at least without the appropriate license, exist in Israeli military orders (still in force), but the Israeli army focuses on pursuing Palestinian militants and activists rather than illegal hunters. Laws regulating hunting from the period Jordan ruled the West Bank (1949–1967) are also still on the books. Neither of these legal instruments have much effect: more salient is the fact that like all sites of conflict, illegal weapons abound in Palestine, smuggled by Israeli and other arms dealers.

The fate of two laws passed by the Palestinian Legislative Council (PLC), our parliament, is sadly instructive. The 132-member body sat for the first time in March 1996, in the wake of the first Palestinian elections. Now silent for a decade as a result of the split in Palestinian governance—between Fatah, the dominant party in the Palestinian Authority in the West Bank, and Hamas, in Gaza—the PLC was active in passing legislation in its first three years. The 1999 Environmental Law has a provision to prohibit the hunting of wild animals and birds, and a 1998 law contains articles on the licensing of firearms and ammunition. Both, however, mandate specific regulations to be issued later, whether a list of prohibited wild animals or of prohibited weapons and instructions for licensing. No clear regulations followed. Shortly after these two laws were passed, the ailing peace process effectively went into terminal decline. In July 2000, the Camp David summit called by President Clinton ended in failure, and Israeli Premier Ehud Barak and Palestinian President Yasser Arafat went home to a rapidly changing political landscape.

Palestine entered the new millennium with a new intifada against the occupation, which swept aside regulative concerns. Palestine and Israel both face a global set of common circumstances leading to declines in wildlife and animal welfare: loss of habitat, poaching, industrial farming, and climate change. It may take a leap to connect the failure of a political summit to the fate of gazelles and other animals in Palestine and Israel. The connection, however, is there. With the human consequences of the escalating conflict so dire—four thousand Palestinians killed by the end of 2005, at least half of them civilians, and about one thousand Israeli Jews, more than half civilians—even the most dedicated animal welfare activists have trouble seeing beyond the suffering of their human communities.

In the last decade, commanders in the Palestinian police and security services have tightened control of their forces, regulating use of their guns and ammunition much more strictly. Imad Atrash is proud that he contributed, several years ago, to lobbying Major General Hazem Atallah, the chief of the Palestinian Police, to issue an edict forbidding his troops to use their arms in hunting, part of a ban on the personal use of official weapons. Nongovernmental organizations were not the only lobbyists. Adala Attireh, the dynamic head of the Palestinian Authority's Environmental Quality Agency, told me that "we raised our voice wherever we could."

Tel Aviv University scientist Yoram Yom-Tov has highlighted a similar, if wider, prohibition by Israeli minister Yitzhak Rabin in the late 1960s, which also came after almost two decades of intensive hunting that threatened gazelle and other animal populations. Shortly after the establishment of the Israeli state, Israeli soldiers (and civilians as well) had begun hunting animals with automatic weapons fired from four-wheel-drive vehicles, a practice that did not stop until Rabin's ban, which came at the request of an eminent Israeli zoologist. Gazelle populations began to recover, and in 1993 Israel sought to further protect them by instituting a ban on any hunting of gazelles, although illegal hunting has continued.

At present, Palestinians are required to register their firearms with the Palestinian police, who will not question how they obtained the weapons. Thus, a Palestinian hunting with an illegal weapon should technically face at least a minor fine. But, as Mazin Qumsiyeh commented, "How can a Palestinian judge fine a Palestinian who says he is hungry?" And at least one very large-scale incident of gazelle hunting, which Imad Atrash termed a "massacre," has gone not only unpunished but unnoticed.

Palestine and Israel can have surprisingly harsh winters; severe snow storms descend on us every couple of years. When I first started working at Birzeit University, we were housed in the compound of the Nasser family, the founders of the University and of the girls' school that had preceded it in 1924. My office was in a hut; the only heating was a small kerosene-burning stove. One especially cold day I stood so near to it that my skirt melted just before I was due to receive a British delegation. My mishap was embarrassing but not fatal. One severe winter storm in January 2015 had more drastic consequences for the vulnerable residents of Gaza. They had already suffered the destruction of Israel's 2014 summer war and faced winter without adequate heating and sometimes with inadequate shelter. Strong winds, heavy rains, and low temperatures caused damage and floods, claiming the lives of three children.

In the West Bank, humans were better off, but other animals were in trouble as the cold continued. Gazelles in the southern West Bank, Imad Atrash told me sadly, were weakened and sought shelter in the many caves above the Dead Sea canyons. There, several hundred were captured by hunters and either slaughtered for food or, Imad speculated a bit more hopefully, kept as pets. The caves were in Area C; Dr. Issa at the Environmental Authority said with quiet pain, "We can do nothing in Area C." I remembered the fawn I had encountered in Deir Ballut and hoped was a family pet. A spark of additional hope came when my friend Jamil Hilal told me that when he was growing up in Beit Sahur, his aunt had a pet fawn in her back garden that he enjoyed watching. One day, the young gazelle, now nearly mature, jumped over the gate and into the surrounding hills.

Like most of the Palestinian public, I had not heard about the hundreds of captured gazelles until Imad gave me the heart-wrenching news some two years later. Whether Palestinian or Israeli, we, like the Jordanian Tourist Board, can easily turn our heads away from our vanishing companions. I wanted to find out if the "protected areas" in the West Bank, nature reserves under some form of Palestinian guardianship, provided any refuge for endangered gazelles. Raja, Bassam, and Adam, Bassam's eight-year-old son, came with me one autumn morning to the southern West Bank to investigate the reserve of Wadi Al-Quff.

Wadi Al-Quff is one of eight Palestinian nature reserves or "protected areas" (*mahimyaat* in Arabic) established or given over to the Palestinian Authority, wholly or in part, under the terms of the Oslo Accords. The reserves are small, as only land partially located in Areas A and B was transferred to the Authority; more than two-thirds of the land of nature reserves remained under exclusive Israeli control. Nonetheless, the Palestinian website dedicated to the eight reserves managed by the Authority describes Wadi Al-Quff, admittedly with more than a touch of hyperbole, as the "Garden of Adam and Eve." The description continued with an interesting wrinkle, perhaps unintentional, as the reader is asked a hypothetical question: "Could it be that Adam and Eve, after being driven from the Garden of Eden, lived in the area of Wadi Al-Quff?" *Ah*, I thought, *after* the Garden of Eden, when Adam and Eve were in somewhat dire straits; this sounds like more familiar Palestinian territory. The website also cited the presence of mountain gazelles, along with striped hyenas and an array of smaller animals; I hoped this was not hyberbole.

As we drove through Wadi Al-Nar, the Valley of Fire, I could spy occasional flocks of goats and sheep grazing on its steep hills, which were bone dry before the coming of the autumn rains. Adam pointed his finger out the window and succinctly said in English, "desert, desert." Alas, as we climbed toward the container checkpoint where the road winds up to Beit Sahur, Adam employed another double description. Pointing to a strip of green below, he proclaimed: "garbage, garbage." We could smell it: sewage from Jerusalem with scattered garbage dumped alongside.

Bassam, a sensitive seeker of the quiet beauties of the Palestinian landscape, refused to take the main Highway 60, aptly called a settler road, and turned onto the old road to Hebron, winding us through orchards and small Palestinian villages. Circling around the bustling city of Hebron, we arrived at the three forested hills southwest of the city that constitute the Wadi Al-Quff reserve. An area of about nine hundred acres, the reserve at first glance offered a breathing space in our congested lives. The entrance, however, was discouraging. An unpaved road leading to the Al Safa (Bat) Cave was lined with garbage, not only the ubiquitous plastic bottles and picnic detritus but blackened industrial waste and two corpses of black goats. We decided not to proceed on the "garbage path" to the much-touted cave and instead ascended to one of the hilltops. We thus missed sighting the more than a hundred Egyptian fruit bats that dwell in the cave, but I have to admit to suffering from some species prejudice, so the omission was not particularly painful.

As we walked up through the forest, the tall cypresses and pines and the low-lying Mediterranean oak trees were pleasant, the white-crowned black wheatears flew high overhead, and garbage was limited to a few cardboard coffee cups and plastic bottles along the route. The trail was occasionally marked by the red-and-white signs indicating a "red trail" that the Israeli Nature and Parks Authority often used. At first I thought they were left over from when Israel controlled this area, but looking more carefully, the red was a slightly different color, the paint had dripped in a rather informal way, and the signs petered out, as though the painter had wearied or donor support for sign painting had ended. "It's our guys," I said to Bassam, who concurred and took a picture.

An autumn midmorning and a noisy party of four, including a voluble eight-year-old, are not optimum conditions for spotting animals. But I wanted to believe the website's statement that mountain gazelles might be somewhere in this attractive setting. But the forest was largely silent; all the noise came from a nearby quarry on the outskirts of the reserve. There was no rustling, no hoof or paw prints, no scat from gazelles or other large mammals. I hoped that the stripped skeletons of the black goats tossed in the garbage at the entrance of the reserve might indicate that a hyena had found a tasty meal. After all, Wadi Al-Quff was the home of the sole sighting of a hyena in Imadeddin Albaba's fifteen-month camera search in 2014–2015.

Mazin Qumsiyeh, the consultant on mammals when the management plan for Wadi Al-Quff was drawn up in 2014, wrote then that no gazelles or large carnivores were detected during the period of the field study, although local inhabitants reported past sightings to him. Replying to my query after our visit to Wadi Al-Quff, Mazin was fairly certain that there are no significant populations of larger mammals at the reserve. Mazin believes that hunting and habitat loss may have driven these animals to remoter or safer locations, citing the southern West Bank's Wadi Fukin as a possible refuge. "Wadi Al-Quff is not a protected area," he wrote to me with some bitterness. Much of the land around Wadi Al-Quff—including its own southern slopes—is in Area C, making an integrated strategy for protection extremely difficult. Still there is hope: in our conversation, Dr. Issa, of Palestine's Environmental Quality Agency, confirmed a sighting of a group of gazelles at the reserve in June 2017. I can understand Mazin's bitterness given his enormous efforts to study and preserve Palestine's wildlife: he told me when I visited the museum that "I don't want to document something that will be gone." Still, I am heartened that, on a recent June day, gazelles wandered through the forests of Wadi Al-Quff: that is a fact to hold onto.

Despite the pleasures of our forest walk, Wadi Al-Quff is surrounded by human encroachments. "The noise of the quarry must scare off the animals," Raja, who is very sensitive to noise, commented. He was right: the May 2014 Management Plan for Wadi Al-Quff cited precisely this danger, adding that the quarry was an illegal, unlicensed enterprise far too close to the reserve. Its removal was a major goal "by the end of 2014." Three years later, as 2017 draws to a close, the quarry is still in operation, even on a Friday—although I learned later from Adala Attireh that the Environmental Agency and a number of Palestinian ministries are pursuing a case against the unlicensed quarry in the courts.

We also saw some construction on the southern side of the reserve, and we wondered: the beginnings of yet another factory that will intimidate the animals? As we left Wadi Al-Quff, we noticed stones at the entrance marked with graffiti opposing this new industrial project. Red-inked graffiti declares: "No to industrial facilities" and "Al-Abed facility will not pass." Opposition, even if anonymous. But these rocks are a scene of debate. One graffiti read: "Our health and our environment are more important than capital," an encouraging message. But "more important than capital" is crossed out and replaced with "are with Al-Abed." More threatening is the sign "Al-Abed homeland guards." Once again, Dr. Adala Attireh and Dr. Issa at the Environmental Agency enlightened me. They were proud that the agency had successfully lobbied for a presidential decree against the "Al-Abed facility," in fact a proposed cement factory. But at the moment, that case is also in the courts, as Al-Abed is suing President Mahmoud Abbas. Nothing is easy, and even with a court ruling, enforcement can be difficult, whether it opposes the "Al-Abed homeland guards" or a quarry owner with powerful connections. I remembered the head of the Palestinian police's criminal investigation unit in Hebron telling me a few years ago that his officers could not even enter the area of the Old City where settlers live (called H2) to pursue Palestinian criminals who shelter there.

Despite its website advertisement, Wadi Al-Quff is inhabiting an age decidedly after the Garden of Eden. There is no return to that mythical garden or to the landscapes of the past. Those who protest human incursions into our remaining protected areas, whether opposing an illegal quarry or illegal hunting, are beleaguered. Perhaps poets can offer the vision we need for a new approach. In his poem "If I Were a Hunter," Mahmoud Darwish evokes a hunter of gazelles seeking companionship rather than slaughter:

> If I were a hunter
> I'd give the gazelle
> a chance and another,
> and a third, and a tenth,
> to doze a little. My share
> of the booty would be peace of mind
> under her dozing head.

The declining gazelle population—including the "uncounted" gazelles of the West Bank, now probably numbering fewer than a thousand—illuminates the problem of understanding the lives and prospects of the wild creatures in a land that is crisscrossed with human barriers, both physical and ideological, and where "capital," occupation, and conflict supersede both human and animal welfare. But the long significance of gazelles to humans in Palestine and the Near East has not vanished. Examining and reflecting on the Chalcolithic (Copper) Period–remains of 268 gazelles found at Marj Rabba in the Galilee during a 2009–2014 excavation, four American archeologists and anthropologists, Max Price, Austin Hill, Yorke Rowan, and Morag Kestrel, wondered about the economic and symbolic role of gazelles in this period (when hunting had decreased with the advent of agriculture but, surprisingly, rituals surrounding gazelles seem to have intensified). Burned feet and other intentionally destroyed parts of gazelles at the site suggested ritual use. They argue that the long history of interactions between humans and gazelles in the Near East is replete with symbolic associations with flight and transition, including the transition from life to death, associations that gave gazelles magical qualities. They ended their analysis of ancient remains with an urgent contemporary plea, writing that "Gazelles have long helped humans muster the courage to face death's twilight; we should repay that debt by bringing them back from the brink of annihilation."

It is this note of repayment, what Darwish calls giving "a chance and another, and a third, and a tenth," that strikes me as I try to understand the situation of gazelles and, more briefly, two other mammals that are still wild: the magnificent ibexes that inhabit the Dead Sea canyons and the less popular gray Arabian wolves, now concentrated in the Israeli-occupied Golan Heights and on the eastern slopes above the Dead Sea, with a scattering in the Upper Galilee.

Perhaps I should stop heeding the news. Last summer, Raja boycotted reading the news from Palestine and Israel for a month and became a much more cheerful person. But I can't stop. Just the other day, I clicked once again to discover that the ibexes of the Dead Sea wadis are in danger not from hunters but from another threat: Dead Sea sinkholes. The Dead Sea, at 1,400 feet below sea level, is the lowest place on our globe and ten times as salty as the ocean. It lies along the Great Rift Valley, a crack in the earth that runs, with slightly different tectonic formations, from Mozambique to eastern Syria. One of the world's wonders, the sea is shrinking rapidly, by about one meter per year. In the Rift's great span of time—it was formed 35 million years ago—the Dead Sea is a newcomer, a mere twelve thousand years old. Other bodies of water have preceded our sea along this stretch of the Rift, most recently the Lisan, which was six times the Dead Sea's size. Perhaps in geological time, another body of water will replace our Dead Sea, but this is as little comfort as the stinging salt of the sea that assaults the eyes of those who try to swim in it rather than float on its surface.

The Dead Sea's only water source except for the winter rains pouring down the wadis is the Jordan River, which flows into its northern reaches. But that once mighty river has become a trickle due to massive diversion for agriculture, upstream damming, and increased water use for other purposes. Israel, Jordan, and Syria are riparian "partners" to the Jordan, but conflict, rather than cooperation, has shadowed the river's course in the last seventy years. The Dead Sea is also threatened by Israeli and Jordanian mineral-extracting industries on its shores, particularly the large Israeli complex in the south, which use vast amounts of its waters and return very little. As the Dead Sea retreats, it leaves behind salt deposits that in turn collapse into large craters, some as deep as 150 feet and twice as wide. These are the sinkholes. They are not always visible, and the ground can simply collapse on the unwary: at least one camel has perished, and several cars have disappeared. One Israeli scientist, trying to count sinkholes around the Ein Gedi kibbutz and reserve, had to be rescued after a twelve hour stint in a hole. Given his circumstances, his count was curtailed; it is estimated that overall there are at least six thousand sinkholes around the Dead Sea. Forty years ago there were none.

I had assumed the ibexes that inhabit the canyons rising above the Dead Sea were immune to the threats facing other wildlife in Palestine and Israel. Aside from a rather unsightly hotel enclave halfway along the western shore of the sea and the mineral industries on the southern shore, human development is scarce, and hunters cannot penetrate the ibexes' favorite wild home at the Ein Gedi Nature Reserve on the western shore of the Dead Sea. But I didn't count on sinkholes.

Ibexes were hunted in the first half of the twentieth century, whether by local hunters or by British Mandate officials, and their numbers declined significantly. Since its establishment by Israel in 1953, the Ein Gedi Nature Reserve has offered a sanctuary where ibexes have been able to survive, although it only became a protected nature reserve in 1971. Ein Gedi is the largest oasis in the country, fed by four springs and featuring waterfalls, cliffs, and ancient ruins. When I first visited Ein Gedi in the 1980s, I walked along the path to the waterfall in a trance; I was bewitched. And then I saw an ibex, the wild goat that haunts these cliffs above the Dead Sea. I gasped at his agility and stately bearing. With the huge curved horns of a mature male—ibexes can live to fourteen years or so—he sported a beard that looked freshly trimmed. The Nubian ibex (*Capra nubiana*) is an agile climber, with hooves that can both grip rocky surfaces and serve as shock absorbers when the goat takes those astounding cliffside leaps. Few other grazing animals possess the ibex's dexterity, which leaves the grasses and shrubs on the high cliffs for its sole delectation; the ibex's penchant for heights also partially protects it from predators. Only particularly nimble hunters, such as wolves and, before their demise in the Dead Sea area, Arabian leopards, can sometimes track an Ibex to these heights. Although sociable animals, male and female ibexes live separately most of the year, Hinson points out, with males entering battle shortly before the rutting season, a time when male and female herds combine.

The beauty of Ein Gedi has struck many a traveler besides myself. The Scottish theologian George Adam Smith, traveling to Palestine in the early twentieth century, marveled: "He who has been to Engedi will always fear lest he exaggerate its fertility to those who have not." And Tristram in his 1866 exploratory survey of fauna could hardly stop counting the wildlife he found around this desert oasis, as he excitedly noted many tracks of leopards, wolves, hyenas, and other large animals.

Travelers in the centuries before Smith and Tristram's time rarely traversed the Dead Sea as far as Ein Gedi, although the oasis was inhabited in Chalcolithic times five thousand years ago: the ruins of a temple from that era still guard a steep hilltop. An intact mosaic floor from a Jewish synagogue of the third century attests to human presence in the Byzantine period, when the waters of Ein Gedi supported agriculture, particularly date palms. Balsam, that precious crop for perfume and medicine, was said to grow in Ein Gedi, as it was in Jericho. Myth has it that balsam was a gift from the Queen of Sheba to King Solomon, brought from Arabia, an account tourist guides in Ein Gedi still tell—although balsam, a desert tree with white blossoms, could be indigenous to the area. That King Herod really gave one balsam grove along the Dead Sea to Cleopatra has at least a ring of historical truth.

But from medieval times onward, accounts of the region were replete with warnings of the horrors of Dead Sea travel, and Ein Gedi lapsed into obscurity. Barbara Krieger's lively and learned account has choice examples from across the centuries as pilgrims, explorers, and pundits, whether they had been to the Dead Sea or not, cited its poisonous vapors and monstrous serpents. These fears were fueled, Krieger notes, by Biblical visions of the fate of Sodom and Gomorrah, whose ruins, in some imaginings, sat at the bottom of the sea, making it the very "mouth of Hell." The Dead Sea has served as a mirror for the human imagination even for those who did not glimpse the cities of the plain below its surface. My favorite example is the gloomy Herman Melville, who reached the Dead Sea in 1856, miserable from the negative reception of *Moby Dick*. He wrote in his travel diary: "Ride over mouldy plain to Dead Sea . . . carried the bitter in my mouth all day — bitterness of life . . . Bitter is it to be poor & bitter . . . & Oh bitter are these waters of Death, thought I."

Today, travelers flock to the Dead Sea for its healing powers rather than its awe-inspiring horrors or melancholy bitterness. Celebrating a family wedding on the Jordanian side of the Dead Sea in September, I floated on a turquoise sea with French, Italian, and American visitors, along with Jordanian and Palestinian friends. I looked across at our western side, the mountains stained with pink. It seemed like Paradise. But it is a sad contradiction that as the Dead Sea's reputation for human pleasure and health increases, its existence is threatened.

A month later, on a cool Sunday morning, Raja and I decided to return to Ein Gedi. The sea was once again turquoise, turning to pale blue at its edges, and the mountains of Moab on the Jordanian side glowed pink in the morning sun. But red signs along the way read DANGER!, warning motorists not to turn down a deserted road or leave their cars to descend to the shore. They look eerily like the signs posted at the entrance to Palestinian towns and villages in the West Bank warning Israelis not to enter Palestinian communities, citing "risk to life." In several places, road diversions skirt old patches of road that can no longer be used because of sinkholes. I try to see the site of the former Ein Gedi beach, a favorite public area for picnics and Dead Sea soaks, frequented by both Palestinian and Israeli families in the 1980s, before both checkpoints and sinkholes. It is now a desolate stretch of shore that no one can approach.

We walk along a road connecting the entrances to the two canyons in the Ein Gedi reserve to inspect the date palm plantations where many ibexes, especially in the hot summer months, graze on grasses and shrubs. Sinkholes had appeared near these plantations, and a newspaper headline sounded an alarm: "Sinkholes threatening existence of Israeli ibex near Dead Sea." The threat was not just the sinkholes themselves but the fencing the Israel Land Authority proposed around the plantations in light of possible sinkhole dangers, a project opposed by the Nature and Parks Authority, which worried that ibexes would no longer be able to access this important food source. Raja and I argued amiably along the way about whether the fencing we saw was new or old, whether the road had always been there, and whether the date palms were being tended or not. The first issue was quickly resolved by a park ranger who told me that the fence was still not built. "From ancient times, the ibexes have fed under the date palms," he commented, adding that "It is good for agriculture." While it is true that ibexes are good for agriculture, spreading seeds with their scat and keeping weeds under control, the ranger's appeal to ancient times was significant. Ibexes have indeed

been around Ein Gedi for a very long time, nourishing both
the valuable balsam and the more lowly date palms with their
scat. In this contested land, ancient presence, for humans as
well as ibexes, is often called upon as a claim of ownership.

Naming, too, can often be claiming. Israel calls the main Ein
Gedi canyon Wadi David, after King David, who, according to
the Bible, "dwelt in the strongholds of Ein Gedi" while hiding from King Saul. The British-based Palestine Exploration
Fund marked the canyon on its maps with its Arabic appellation, Wadi Sidar, derived from the jujube tree (Christ's Thorn)
that grows along the stream. *It is a relief,* I thought as we walked
along, *that Ein Gedi itself simply means the spring of the young goat
in both Arabic and Hebrew.* We moved quickly away from the
entrance, hoping to get ahead of an amazing number of Israeli
teenagers descending from their buses on school expeditions.
In the few minutes of silence, we encountered another of the
wild animals of the unique Dead Sea zone, sunning itself on a
rock—a rock hyrax or coney, a remote ancestor of the elephant.
Although this small animal looks like a cross between a rodent
and a rabbit, it occupies a separate order among the family of
odd-toed ungulates, which includes elephants, rhinoceros, and
horses. Hyraxes pop out of rocky crevasses all along the Jordan
Valley and share the cliffs of Ein Gedi with ibexes. Indeed,
a line from Psalm 104 is frequently evoked in describing Ein
Gedi: "The high mountains are for the wild goat [i.e., ibexes],
the rocks are for the conies." Today, hyraxes, like jackals, are
adapting and moving closer to human settlements. Ibexes,
however, cannot find secure refuge on their high cliffs. It is
not only the sinkholes of the Dead Sea that threaten them.
The Separation Wall is moving ever closer to the Dead Sea
and its canyons. Though parts of the Wall along the approved
southern route are not built yet or are under construction, the

completed Wall would curtail the circulation these wild creatures need for survival.

One of the natural predators of the ibex around Ein Gedi,
the Arabian leopard, has been declared extinct on more than
one occasion. Another predator, the Arabian wolf, has survived
better. The Arabian leopard (*Panthera pardus nimr*) was the
arch-predator of the Judean wilderness and desert. Its range
was wide: Tristram, in his observations from the 1860s, noted
leopards in the Dead Sea, Gilead, Bashan, and even the hills
above Haifa where he observed, without any further comment,
"I found a fine pair which had been killed on Mount Carmel."
The killing of this fine pair was not a lone incident; many more
of their kind perished as hunting continued unchecked. But, on
a (slightly) hopeful note, leopards in Palestine have repeatedly
been declared extinct only to surface again.

An Israeli zoologist, Giora Ilani, working for the Nature
Reserve Authority around Ein Gedi in the 1970s and 1980s,
was determined to save the remaining leopards that inhabited the canyons above the Dead Sea. However, Ilani may
inadvertently have led these big cats "down the road to ruin,"
according to Alon Tal. Ilani was no moderate in his passion
for leopards and other animals in the unique habitation of the
Dead Sea and Rift Valley. Indeed, he advocated zero human
habitation along the valley. Ilani left food for leopards in the
area, gave them names, monitored their lives, and, in short,
loved these magnificent cats with their black spots and tails
that are almost as long as their bodies. But residents of Kibbutz
Ein Gedi were regularly losing domestic cats, as well as several
sheep from their petting zoo, to poaching leopards. An elec-
tric fence erected in 1982 by the Nature Reserves Authority
failed to stop leopard incursions. The list of complaints grew:
leopards might frighten tourists at the kibbutz's hotels and

they might bring disease. Then the old antagonism between humans and other predators took a deadly turn, as kibbutz residents resorted to strychnine, traps, and hunting.

In 1992, a survey found no leopards in the wilderness above the Dead Sea. When I was first in Palestine, there was still an occasional rumor of a living, if aged, leopard in the area. And although Tal was sure none remain in the Jerusalem wilderness and Ein Gedi, a lone male leopard surfaced in 2017 south of the Dead Sea. Five years earlier, a surveillance camera mounted on the Wall in the northern West Bank captured an image of another. A lone male leopard does not signal species survival. Indeed, like lionesses, female leopards are the main hunters and thus the main target for human action; they may have vanished before their male counterparts. Still, in the Naqab (Negev) Desert, some say there may be as many as ten leopards. However, a dedicated team of volunteers searching for them with camera posts over the past five years has yet to sight one. The Arabian leopard remains critically endangered.

I wondered if the gray wolf (*Canis lupus*), once the most widely distributed large mammal in the world, and its smaller subspecies, the Arabian wolf (*Canis lupus arabs*), which inhabits the southern desert, was also in trouble on our small patch of ground. I had heard of only one recent sighting of wolves of any stripe in the West Bank, where a pair were spotted to the north near Jenin in 2016. On the highest hill in the Galilee, Mount Meron (Jabal Jarmak in Arabic), a photo of two wolves taken at night that same year reduced them to shadows with glittering eyes. Wolves are protected in the nature reserves of the Golan Heights, but cattle ranchers on Israeli settlements in the southern part of the region are allowed to kill them, although poison is forbidden. Despite this—and even with the leftover minefields from the 1973 war, when Israel occupied this Syrian territory—wolves seem to be doing better in the Golan than in most areas of Israel proper. Naqab (Negev) Desert also has a small wolf population.

I speculated that the profusion of jackals in the West Bank signaled that wolves might be dwindling to very small numbers. Wolves are apex predators and might not be prone to coexist with quite so many jackals. But Imad Atrash contradicted my attempt at wildlife logic. "I saw wolves near the container," he said, using one of the new Palestinian geographic markers, this one a container checkpoint on the edge of the Jerusalem wilderness. Imad's estimate of the number of wolves was in the hundreds, mostly, he thought, on the eastern slopes toward the Jordan Valley and Dead Sea. Another Palestinian wildlife expert would not give a number, commenting there has been no count of any kind, so I must remain puzzled. In his survey in the 1880s, Tristram called the wolf "common in Palestine," lurking "during the day among the rocks" and prowling "during the night among the sheepcotes." He thought that Palestine was probably the southeastern limit of the gray wolf's range.

The name of a Palestinian village on the eastern slopes signaled the presence of wolves, at least in the past. The small community of Jubbet ad-Dhib, whose name means "the pocket of the wolf, " sits at the foot of Herodion, the palace fortress of Herod the Great. Its 170 residents have made repeated requests to be connected to the electricity and water grids, but have always been turned down by the ubiquitous Civil Administration. The reason is simple: they have the bad luck to reside in Area C. Remote and neglected, the village made news in the summer of 2017 when Israeli soldiers seized solar panels that had been donated by the Dutch government. A village in Area C might well be described as in the pocket of the wolf.

Fortunately, the panels were returned the following October, after Dutch protests and a case raised in the Israeli High Court arguing that Israel had violated international law.

Wolves in the eastern wadis near the Dead Sea made both local and international news in September 2017. Instead of the usual headlines about human conflict, a Haaretz headline warned its readers of "Brazen wolves preying on children in Israel's south." The story did instill fear, reporting ten attacks in four months by wolves on Israeli campers and hikers. Several children were bitten, including two near Ein Gedi. Although the children suffered only light injuries, something was happening between humans and wolves that was unusual. The language of the usually staid newspaper was telling; the headline warned of danger to all children in the South, rather than the wounding of several children, and gave wolves a perverse human character by calling them "brazen." As between kibbutzniks and leopards in Ein Gedi, ancient and not so ancient human hatred of a predator rose to the surface. The consequences of this animosity can be dire: in the United States, vigorous extermination campaigns against once-abundant gray wolves led to their near disappearance even though, as Tim Flannery notes, drawing on the study of a very patient scholar, "there is not a single example of a wolf in nature killing a human in the whole history of North America."

One expert on wolf behavior, Dr. Haim Berger, proposed that the wolves living above the Dead Sea had become acclimatized to humans: fifty years ago, he said, wolves would never have approached a Bedouin encampment. Other voices from the Nature and Parks Authority agreed with Berger that human behavior, including feeding wolves and improper storage of food and garbage by campers, was the main problem. Berger also believes a single pack of perhaps twenty wolves—

or indeed just several individual wolves from the pack—were the attackers. An attack on children, even with only light injuries, is certainly alarming. But humans have also mistaken this landscape for something that is theirs alone, rather than a wild place shared with other predators requiring caution and respect.

If Imad Atrash is correct, the southern West Bank may now have slightly more wolves than gazelles, more predators than prey. Our world, we might conclude, is out of balance. We might despair at a diminishing Dead Sea, an unprotected nature reserve at Wadi Al-Quff, a lone leopard, or a massacre of gazelles during a harsh winter. But it was human hands that reduced the Jordan River to a trickle and human hunters who pulled the trigger that cold January on gazelles sheltering in caves. To restore the Jordan River requires extensive political will and regional cooperation. But those of us who can only work on a smaller scale must seek other solutions.

The small urban nature reserve near a busy West Jerusalem intersection was almost deserted on a warm October afternoon. After only a few minutes, I saw her: a fawn lying under a brush of shrubbery, perhaps hidden by her mother after a feeding. And then a mature gazelle, picking her way through a field of autumn-yellow low bushes. A young male, followed by a female, emerged and crossed the path. Although more than half of this sixty-four-acre reserve is roped off from humans, these gazelles are on the side permitted to walkers. Given their sensitive hearing, I wonder if they are simply stunned by the roar of traffic around them. Or, perhaps, in this special place, humans are not feared as predators.

"I can't help it," confessed my friend Rema Hammami, as we

walked along a path with newly planted fruit trees. Her sharp anthropologist's eye was scanning the landscape for traces— such as terraces or the remnants of an old stone house—that would suggest that the valley once was Palestinian village land. That is part of the story of Wadi Gazelle that is absent from the signs giving visitors the post-1948 history of the valley and the animals, birds, and plants that have flourished there. Rema also questioned the frequent mention in signs of the "rehabilitation" of the gazelles: "Are they criminals?" she inquired. Perhaps it is humans that need rehabilitation.

Some humans, in the shape of a local community action committee, had waged a fifteen-year struggle to block plans to develop the valley through a large building project and to save the herd of gazelles living there, then numbering around thirty, a mere fraction of the population that once inhabited the western slopes of Jerusalem. Wadi Gazelle, opened in busy West Jerusalem in 2015, only exists because of those activists who successfully lobbied a powerful municipality. I recall the scrawled graffiti on the stones of Wadi Al-Quff. Palestinian voices, yes, but at the moment with only the power of a spray can. But gazelles roaming a small urban reserve in West Jerusalem give me hope that Wadi Al-Quff, almost ten times the size and a former habitat of gazelles, could one day be a true protected area—once humans are rehabilitated.

Neither Gazelle Valley nor a protected Wadi Al-Quff are adequate substitutes for the contiguous land, ecological corridors, and bans on hunting needed to preserve our indigenous gazelle. Its survival hinges on the will and capacities of both Israelis and Palestinians, and it is hard to envision it occurring under conditions of continued military occupation. It is disturbing but telling that naming, rather than saving, this delicate creature threatened with extinction has become a peculiar human obsession. When a right-wing Israeli hip-hop star (sometimes known as "the Shadow") discovered a sign at a venerable Israeli institution, the Jerusalem Biblical Zoo, that named the "Palestine Gazelle," he fomented a Facebook storm against the "garbage-can geniuses of the left." That name had in fact been given to the mountain gazelle by those fiery radicals, the British Mandatory officials. Genetic variations, admittedly minor, discovered recently in our mountain gazelle have contributed to proposals for the name of a new species: the Israeli gazelle. That name is adopted in brochures in English and Hebrew given out at Gazelle Valley. Interestingly, there is a different name in the Arabic text: *baladi* gazelle, or the gazelle of the country, our indigenous compatriot.

Haifa-based artist Manal Mahamid mounted a solo exhibit at a Ramallah art gallery in 2016. In a video accompanying her paintings of gazelles, she holds a white ceramic gazelle with an amputated leg as she walks through valleys and along the coast. A hundred of these statues were posed eerily on the floor below. The most striking of her paintings was a series of gazelles obscured by superimposed urban cityscapes. One of them now graces a wall in our house. I often look at it. The gazelle is almost hidden, but she is there.

THE WORST ZOO IN THE WORLD: LIVES IN COMMON?

In August 2016, Laziz, a Bengal tiger, was transferred by Four Paws, an international animal welfare organization, from the zoo in the southern Gaza city of Khan Yunis—dubbed the "worst zoo in the world"—to the Lionsrock refuge in South Africa. His rescue made world headlines.

Laziz had entered Gaza as a tiger cub smuggled through one of the tunnels under the Egyptian border. His exit, along with five monkeys, an emu, and assorted other animals, was at the request of the zoo owner, who felt he could no longer care for the animals given the harsh conditions in war-ravaged Gaza. He was not alone in this assessment: a previous transfer of two lions to Jordan from a zoo in northern Gaza had occurred in the wake of Israel's 2014 Gaza War. That summer, according to the United Nations, 2,251 Gazans lost their lives, of whom 1,462 were civilians and 551 children. And many animals in Gaza's zoos, as well as on Gaza's streets and fields, also perished from shelling or starvation.

But it took (once again) veteran journalist Amira Hass to zero in on the Orwellian statements of the "chief warden" of besieged Gaza, the Israeli coordinator of government activities in the territories (COGAT). In his press release on the rescue

Shepherd surveys his flock of sheep near Aqraba, northern West Bank. *(Credit: Bassam Almohor)*

of Laziz and his cohorts, the official praised the Israeli government's "concern for the animals" because of their "poor living conditions" and announced they would receive better medical care outside Gaza. "What luck it is to be a tiger" who is allowed freedom of movement, Hass concluded. In contrast, she observed that Gaza's cancer patients often cannot receive permits to leave for treatment, no Gazan product can be exported, and lives continue to be blighted by unemployment, severe environmental problems, and above all, confinement. The worst zoo in the world imprisons humans as well as other animals.

While Laziz—who hopefully is flourishing in his new home in South Africa—is not among the native mammals I have considered in this book, his story highlights one of my chief concerns: the intertwining of our lives with other mammals in this burdened land and the complexities and contradictions that ensue when we are all companions in conflict. Captivity or freedom, well-being or ill-being, adequate or constrained habitat: none are issues concerning humans alone, and yet Gazans have a right to wonder (and, as is their wont, to joke) why Laziz's life is valued over theirs.

This painful contradiction can lead to cynicism among Palestinians about initiatives for animal welfare or wildlife protection. But it could—and sometimes does—lead to a deeper understanding of the common conditions faced by people and other animals in occupied Palestine, whether shrinking habitat or outright conflict and war, conditions not unique to Palestine on our embattled globe. One young woman, Aseel Saleh, a participant in the Palestinian Animal League's Youth for Change initiative, said: "Today we start teaching the new generation the opposite of what we face from occupation." The coordinator of the Youth for Change program, Sameh Arekat, told me that the impulse for the program was breaking the cycle of violence experienced by children and youth, violence from the occupation, the society, and among themselves. They found, he said, that the best way was to "encourage responsibility and compassion towards the weakest beings in the cycle of violence, animals."

To reflect on new approaches to thinking and acting on our common dilemmas, I turn, in this conclusion, both to what I have learned from the animals I have met in this book and to the wisdom and experience of Palestine's environmental, wildlife, and animal welfare activists, now encompassing several generations. "I tell children," said Ahmad, from the Palestinian Animal League, "If Palestine was only its people, we could make Palestine in Brazil. But Palestine is the land, and the animals, and the plants, our whole environment."

Ahmad's call for a wider view of Palestine's "whole environment" is particularly difficult to achieve in the fragmented and isolating context of occupied Palestine. I fully realized this point as I listened to speaker after speaker at a 2016 conference in Bethlehem celebrating the tenth anniversary of the admirable Environmental Education Center in nearby Beit Jala, whose achievements over the decade, particularly with children and young people, are entirely worthy. But as the day progressed, I began to feel claustrophobic. Somehow, I thought, our horizons have shrunk and a disturbing new normal has emerged. No one mentioned Gaza, let alone the Arab region. The Dead Sea and the Mediterranean Sea were absent from our ecologies, as was the Jordan River and the Naqab (Negev) Desert. It might be that the conference participants were simply being practical, focusing on what can actually be done by Palestinian environmental activists in the West Bank, whose terrain, it must be admitted, is limited to the towns, villages, and refugee camps in Areas A and B. Thus, speakers focused on education (the schools are under Palestinian control), on individual behavior, or on municipal efforts to encourage waste reduction and energy conservation.

And then I suddenly noticed another absence. Speaker after speaker invoked the *environment* (*bi'a* in Arabic), a word that seemed to signify a series of problems. Then, one enthusiastic young woman spoke of her wonder at the lovely landscape surrounding the hilltop Palestinian village of Deir Ghassaneh and used the word *nature* (*tabi'a* in Arabic). This old, surely ancient word for the natural world that surrounds us and that we inhabit was invoked frequently when I first encountered the Palestinian landscape in the 1980s and friends invited me to leave the town for an excursion into "nature." What happens when new talk of environment supersedes this rooted notion of nature? Globally, the "end of nature" is both a lament for our continuing losses and a recognition that we are living in a new era, the anthropocene, where human activity is a major force shaping the planet and its ecosystems. I do not dispute this; how could I? Nonetheless, in Palestine and perhaps elsewhere, I think we need to reclaim our *tabi'a*. It is troubling if environment as a problem entirely replaces nature as pleasure. Sitting with shepherds in Zanuta, I listened to their almost insurmountable problems, as this herding community is faced time and time again with demolition orders. But I also looked up at the winter-green southern Hebron Hills and heard a shepherd's happiness at being "far away from urban problems." Delight in our shared world, however endangered, needs to be cherished for itself, as well as a motivation to act for its preservation.

City streets are not the best place to encounter the natural world. In Palestine, however, as I heard from the conference speakers, we often operate when and where we can. A smoky café in Ramallah on an autumn evening hosts a benefit for the Palestinian Animal League. Most of the audience is young, whether internationals or residents. Young Palestinian women wearing hijabs laugh and sip juice drinks, while Ramallah hipsters and foreign visitors drink beer and wine. All are having a convivial time listening to a band led by a musician from Brazil. It's the Ramallah bubble at its best. There are no speeches and no pitches for funds, simply a donation box and the café owner's own commitment to turn over that evening's profits to PAL. Slides flash by on a small screen, highlighting PAL's activities: donkey welfare, rescue of stray dogs and injured cats, a vegan café at Al-Quds University, and an upcoming three-day conference on animal welfare in Palestine. The slides are in English, not unusual for a Palestinian NGO, where international connections are a lifeline, but the absence of Arabic gives me pause. Then a slide flashes by for an activity I hadn't come across before: "Come with PAL for a Friday dog run," it read. I had often driven past a small pet shop on one of Ramallah's main arteries and heard miserable dogs barking from their small cages. Every Friday, it seems, some are released for a few hours of exercise with PAL volunteers. Perhaps another mirror of Palestinian life in our current period: we live in a cage and give ourselves a few breaths of fresh air through cultural expression, social media activism, or an occasional walk in a wadi or along a forest trail in a nature reserve. And then, both people and animals return to their cages.

Environmental historian Shaul Cohen has argued that in both Israel and Palestine nationalism trumps environmentalism. Although he acknowledges the unequal relations between the two parties, his framework of contending nationalisms does not allow us to address these caged lives and the questions of justice that are urgent for the lives and futures of both

Palestinians and Israelis. Common lives, I think, must mean a common struggle both against Israel's occupation and for the future of the land that both peoples inhabit, along with all its living creatures. This future cannot be secured while one people oppresses another and while we live in a cage. And that, I would argue, is the major contradiction trumping environmentalism. This does not mean there is no informal cooperation on environmental and animal protection issues across the Wall: a Tel Aviv zookeeper sent Dr. Sami at the Qalqilya zoo two giraffes, who perished when a more formal institutional presence in the shape of the Israeli army entered the town. Another Israeli colleague took care of the hyena Imad Atrash rescued at an oasis near Jericho. And Israelis, Jordanians, and Palestinians work together through EcoPeace on a Dead Sea project to save what can be saved of the shrinking sea. Still, young Palestinians, like my nephew Aziz's pals in Ramallah, are incredulous at international outrage at the death of a donkey when they have suffered from the siege of their city. And Gazans come out to say a fond farewell to Laziz the lion but also wonder when they will have the right to move across borders.

Ahmad Safi, a committed vegan and the founder of Palestine's first vegan café, published a telling intervention in 2016 when the Israeli army made headlines and received global praise from animal rights organizations for accommodating vegan soldiers with special menus, non-leather boots, and non-wool clothing. Ahmed expressed his bafflement when he heard a radio interview with a young vegan soldier; the commentator noted that "her diet is so important to her that had the army not been able to provide conditions that had harmed no living creature, she might not have enlisted in a combat union." Ahmed's cogent comment: "The only way I can interpret this is that the soldier in question does not consider Palestinians to be living creatures." He added a personal note from his experience growing up in Jalazoun refugee camp:

> I am someone who, myself, was beaten so badly by a sergeant in the Israeli army when I was ten years old that I coughed up blood from internal injuries. Would my experience, or that of my friends, family, fellow countrymen and women be different if the boot that kicked me was vegan, or the hat on the sniper's head who took my uncle's life was made from polyester, not wool?

Ahmad and the vegan soldier are on different sides, even if both are sincerely committed to animal rights. And these sides are not simply two nationalisms or two ideologies; the vegan soldier is actively engaged in an army which oppresses Ahmad and all Palestinians under occupation. I recall a remark by Rita Giacaman, my longtime friend and colleague at Birzeit University. We had gathered at a hilltop restaurant near Beit Jala to celebrate the eighty-fifth birthday of our cherished companion Judy Blanc, a founder of the Israeli Friends of Birzeit University and of Women in Black, a resolute anti-occupation movement of Israeli women. "People ask me how Judy and I, Israeli and Palestinian from different sides, manage to work together. I say, but Judy and I are on the same side," Rita said, raising her glass in a toast. Judy and Rita are on the same side not simply out of sentiment, but in shared action. And indeed, we were celebrating not only Judy's birthday but also her nineteen-year-old grandson's release from prison after serving eight terms for refusing to serve in the Israeli army because of his objection to occupation. Natan, by the way, is a committed vegan.

Palestinians and Israelis also live under the shared shadow of global climate crisis, acutely evident in our land in less rainfall (or variability in rainfall), shorter winters, and the threat of another major drought in the region, or indeed a major earthquake along the Rift Valley faults. Are we so absorbed in our conflict, and for Palestinians, in the burdens of occupation, that we fail to address these present and coming crises? I went to Palestine's first conference on climate change to see. Conferences are not the most thrilling of events for either participants or readers, and I hesitate to describe another one, but Palestine has become the land of conferences, perhaps because our international donors find them one of the easiest "products" for funding. We are now all experts at producing folders, pens, bags, agendas, PowerPoint presentations (this took a while), and logos. The admirable Muwatin (Citizen) Institute for Democracy and Human Rights has been holding an annual conference since the establishment of the Palestinian Authority. Sometimes Raja and I joke that attendance is one of our rituals. "Where to Palestine?" is not always literally the title, but it is certainly the spirit of each discussion. The question remains unanswered.

Conference cynicism aside, it was heartening, in the spring of 2017, to see busloads of engineers, many of them young women, arrive from all over the West Bank to attend this first major discussion on Palestine and climate change, organized by the Association of Engineers. They descended at the imposing Palestine Red Crescent building named after Fathi Arafat, the brother of Yasser Arafat. Its shadow is cast over the low-lying cement dwellings of Amari refugee camp; in 2005, as it was being built, I talked to young people in the camp who protested: "And now we have no sun." Yet another contradiction in our flawed landscape.

The master of ceremonies gravely listed the roll call of climate change issues that need action: carbon emissions from

industry and energy use, rising temperatures, less rain leading to regional drought. "Palestine is not an exception" in the
global effects of climate change, he aptly noted. He went on
to stress, however, that Palestine is an exception as the only
country still under occupation after half a century. The dialec-
tic of exceptional circumstances versus global participation ran
through the conference. We stood to honor the ongoing strike
of Palestinian political prisoners, and then the conference
chair lauded Palestine's April 2016 signing of the Paris Agreement on climate change, while calling on Israel to respect all
international agreements and end the occupation. A video clip
began with "no life without water" and then went on to discuss water shortages and desertification along with the Wall
and the war in Gaza—all threatening "this land and what is
worth living." The only mention of our animal companions
in this shifting environment flashed by: a gazelle "threatened
with extinction." And then a Palestine sunbird, with the same
message, even though this diminutive bird is not in immediate
danger. As I write, a male sunbird, with a flash of turquoise,
is sipping nectar from the yellow trumpet vine in our garden.

Just back from the Basel conference on climate change,
Adala Attireh of the Palestinian Environmental Agency told
us that the Palestinian Authority and leadership have decided
that it is a national priority to join the global effort against climate change. When Adala lists achievements to date, including
Palestine's participation in a number of international fora and
agreements, I recognize a familiar Palestinian politics of presence. We exist, Palestine says; we demand recognition. This
political project, however salient, can consume much of the
energy of Palestinian leaders. Sadly, the only practical project
Adala mentioned was a solar installation supported by Belgium,
launched and then stopped by Israel because it was in Area C.

An American environmental scholar, Stephen Gasteyer was the first of the speakers to explicitly put forward climate justice, spurred not only by his work in Palestine over the years but by his recent involvement in the struggle to reverse the toxic water supply in Flint, Michigan, a community where many are poor and black. He proposed Palestine as a metaphor for climate injustice, citing Israel's policy of designating nature reserves allegedly to protect wildlife and stating that, in reality, that policy is designed to take land out of Palestinian production and declare it state land. The state of course being Israel. Stephen was referring to the large tracts of land in Area C that Israel has designated as reserves, and his point is acute. Land grabs have indeed been a key Israeli strategy during the half century of occupation. Almost a quarter of a century after the signing of the Interim Agreements (Oslo Accords), it is painful to excavate the moribund Article 26 on nature reserves, which reads:

> In Area C, powers and responsibilities related to the sphere of Nature Reserves will be transferred gradually to Palestinian jurisdiction that will cover West Bank and Gaza Strip territory except for the issues that will be negotiated in the permanent status negotiations, during the further redeployment phases, to be completed within 18 months from the date of the inauguration of the Council.

The Council, or Palestinian Authority, was inaugurated in 1996, two decades ago, and, as noted in the previous chapter, to date none of the Area C nature reserves (constituting 80 percent of the West Bank's protected reserves) have been transferred. In examining the large issues of Israeli policy, Stephen did not consider the fate of the smaller reserves under Palestinian control, but I think that challenges to both Israeli policy and improvements to Palestinian practice need to go hand in hand.

Visiting the smallest of the Palestinian nature reserves, Umm al-Tut in the northern West Bank, I tell Bassam's five-year-old daughter Salma, a favorite walking companion, to hold her nose, as the entrance to the reserve is littered not only with garbage but with corpses of a horse, a black goat, and a wild boar. But then we walk up a trail through a lovely forest of native oak and pistachio to the top of a hill. "Across the road is Area C," Ayoub, a biologist from nearby Jenin, tells us, pointing to another forested area. The problems of preserving Umm al-Tut are many: the mountain gazelles and hyenas listed on the reserve's one rusty sign are long gone, although the reserve still hosts many migrating birds. "Nobody cares," Ayoub says bitterly. What would happen, I wonder, if these hills were not divided and the reserve could expand "across the road."

Eight of these very limited nature reserves are under Palestinian authority, and one of them, Wadi Gaza, an important coastal wetland, is highly at risk from toxic contamination. While challenging the larger policies of the occupation and the fragmentation of territory, can we preserve what is at least partially in our hands?

Palestine/Israel remains at the crossroads of three continents, and its small size belies its diverse environments and rich biodiversity. Small size of course amplifies any loss of habitat, whether caused by the Wall that will stretch 403 miles upon completion, dividing and scarring the land, the sprawl from Israeli settlements and Palestinian towns, or a toxic spring. But our very small size may also be one of our advantages in protecting our companions in conflict. Globally, the scale of our problems can paralyze us: loss of insects, loss of fish, loss of large mammals, loss of clean water and air. Locally, we also face losses that, unlike the flow of gloomy global data, we cannot always measure: we know several large mammals— gazelles, hyenas, ibexes—are endangered, but we put hope in our "uncounted gazelles," or the lone sighting of a hyena in Wadi Al-Quff, or a leopard huddled near the Wall. The leaching of biodiversity in Palestine's environments surrounds us, but we fail to comprehend its extent: one of the few detailed local studies, conducted by scholars at the Palestine Museum of Natural History, examined the diet of eagle owls. Their findings suggested a decline in biodiversity, but it was a study of only one wadi near Bethlehem. The wider view of Palestine eludes us. But we hope that Palestinian environmental scholars will contribute to our understanding, and that activists will face our losses with a determination to make a change.

Even though Palestine is indeed no exception to these global crises, the smaller scale we inhabit on our patch of land offers opportunities for action. In Palestine, one person can make a difference. The first native Palestinian zoologist, Dr. Sana Atalla of Beit Sahur, was born in 1943 and lived only twenty-seven years before his death in a car accident. But it is no coincidence that four major environmental and animal welfare organizations came from Beit Sahur, almost literally in his footsteps. Mazin Qumsiyeh is Dr. Atalla's nephew and accompanied him on his field explorations. Imad Atrash of the Palestine Wildlife Society, Simon Awad of the Environmental Education Center, and Jad Ishaq of ARIJ, a major research organization on Palestine's natural resources, are all from Beit Sahur and were all touched by the example of their compatriot. Through law, activism, and community education, our small nature reserves, now largely unprotected, can receive at least our guardianship. The herd of gazelles sighted at Wadi Al-Quff one summer day may wander more freely if the illegal quarry is removed, if more rangers are trained to patrol and protect the reserves, and if our communities are engaged in both enjoying these reserves and contributing to their development and protection. "People can learn," Dr. Issa at the Environmental Agency told me, giving the example of villagers in the Hebron area—near where those fearful Palestinian young men, several years ago, stoned a hyena to death—calling the Hebron office of the agency to rescue a wounded hyena.

The activists I have encountered labor under no illusions about the natural—and cultural—devastation we face. Mazin Qumsiyeh spoke for many when he told me he didn't want to only document what is lost. Nonetheless, their work is infused with an intangible asset which I would call radical hope, after the psychoanalyst and philosopher Jonathan Lear. He discusses radical hope in the face of present devastation, what critic Terry Eagleton has called "hope without optimism," or hope within a present that seems unbearable.

Artists can help us make these imaginative leaps into possible futures. It is telling that the Palestinian Museum of Natural History and Biodiversity founded by Qumsiyeh is not the first of its kind. A conceptual artist from Ramallah, Khalil Rabah, has "operated" the fictional Palestinian Museum of Natural History and Humankind for the past two decades. In 2004, I sat in a Ramallah community center for the "Third Annual Wall Auction." An auctioneer, historian Nazmi Jubeh, with a wide smile above his pert bow tie, auctioned off pieces of the Separation Wall (then just beginning construction) to an eager audience. The calls from the crowd were spirited; we were bidding, it seemed, on a better tomorrow.

Acts of environmental imagination can also contribute to reviving a desolated landscape, whether resurrecting memories, preserving what is left, or envisioning possible futures. In the autumn of 2017, a small bus carried us less than ten miles from Ramallah to Jaba, a village that sits on the edge of the Jerusalem wilderness, below the sprawling Qalandia refugee camp. It also sits directly under a large quarry, which spreads its stone dust over the village's dwellings and olive trees. Raja and I, like most others in Ramallah, had never visited Jaba. For us, it was the name of a checkpoint on the main road above the village. Jaba's own entrance to that bustling road has been blocked for many years.

We entered a lovely *hoash*, a cluster of old buildings recently renovated by Riwaq, a Ramallah-based NGO, and currently the home of an active youth group from Jaba, Qalandia camp, and other nearby communities. Along the walls of the meeting room, photos, drawings, and a sound installation trace a trail taken by young walkers from Jaba to Kafr Aqab on the outskirts of Ramallah. Once a village, Kafr Aqab is now an unwanted and neglected part of the expanded Jerusalem municipality, dense with new (and often unlicensed) buildings. The walkers were reclaiming a forgotten landscape.

Some of the animals I encounter in this book are ghosts in this ravaged landscape. The hints of beauty the walkers have captured in their photos and drawings lie mainly in spring plants, rock formations, and nesting birds. Hyenas once prowled near Kafr Aqab; gazelles, even in my time here, sought spring green in the stony landscape. Herds of sheep and goats still do the same, although they make their way over garbage and sewage. Still, not all has been lost. Memories of the past and a damaged present fuse with an imagined future, another version of radical hope. A geographer from Birzeit University, Omar Imseeh Tesdell, walked this trail of the imagination and came upon an orchard of olive trees near Kafr Aqab. He wrote:

Each tree was an institution. Perhaps it was the walk in the hot May sun over rugged terrain. Perhaps it was seeing the unchecked Palestinian urban expansion and the unchecked Israeli settlement expansion. Knowing how much these trees had survived on this gentle slope below Kafr Aqab. Olive trees are survivors. These trees had survived shifts. They survive civilizations that come and go. They were planted by humans but can survive without humans. What will they have to survive in the next shift?

Can our encounters with gazelles, ibexes, or wolves in the pockets of wilderness left in Palestine encourage us see their survival in the future? The whispers of animals that have become nearly extinct in this land offer a small measure of hope. The Arabian leopard whose image is frozen on a surveillance camera near the Wall, or sighted only once in a steep wadi, may indeed be the last of his kind unless action is taken to reintroduce this most elegant of predators. And it is not too late to learn to, in the words of Mahmoud Darwish, "give the gazelle a chance and another, and a third, and a tenth." The chance, of course, is also our chance not to be abandoned to species loneliness.

I wandered through a major exhibit at the Wellcome Collection in London in 2017; "Making Nature: How We See Animals" explored our vision of animals through photography, taxidermy, and literature. In an evocative video installation we not only saw animals but heard them speaking to us. Artists Allora and Calzadolla screened footage from a sanctuary for endangered parrots in Puerto Rico alongside a video of Puerto Rico's Arecibo Observatory, which transmits messages into outer space in search of extraterrestrial intelligence.

The parrots speak to us:

The humans use Arecibo to look for extraterrestrial intelligence. Their desire to make a connection is so strong that they've created an ear capable of hearing across the universe. But I and my fellow parrots are right here. Why aren't they interested in listening to our voices? We're a nonhuman species capable of communicating with them. Aren't we exactly what humans are looking for?

Like the parrots in Puerto Rico, the animals in this book are right here beside us. Thinking of all the mammals—including humans—I have met along the way in my time in Palestine, I consider that hard question: What conditions do we need, for humans as well as other mammals, for our common lives in Palestine/Israel to flourish? The answer cannot be mine alone, and it is time to listen to the animals I encountered. I have learned from Abu Hassan, the hyena caught in a trap, that the hunter can fear the hunted—and the occupier the occupied. In a small, fragmented, and contested land, we all, humans and animals, suffer from loss of habitat. I have learned from Kojak the camel that we can all be driven to the point of madness by the maze of restrictions that we endure. I have learned that an ancient way of life—shepherds with their flocks—survives, even if its communities are under threat, and that we would all suffer were they to vanish from our landscape. Amer Shomali's animated cows provided pungent comments on an unusual story of Palestinian resistance, while the relatively small-scale industrial dairy enterprise of Juneidi in Hebron led me to think of the confined lives of these "modern" cows even as I understand the impulse for Palestinian economic development. I have learned that those animals who are the most like us in their ability to adapt, survive, and even thrive amid our garbage and detritus—jackals and wild boars—will persist and indeed flourish. But I also know that our lives and futures would be radically impoverished if mountain gazelles no longer picked their way up our stone terraces and down the wadis, or if ibexes no longer stood high on the cliffs above the Dead Sea.

The stories that have been told for millennia about all these animals—from hypnotic hyenas to Adonis and the wild boar, to Kafka's jackals, to Mahmoud Darwish's vision of a sleeping gazelle, to newspaper headlines pronouncing cooperation between wolves and hyenas in the Naqab (Negev) Desert as an image of Middle East peace—attest to how our companions are interwoven in our imaginations as well as our lives. And I have also learned from the wisdom of donkeys and the whispers from the wild, as well as from a new generation of Palestinian environmental activists, that there are other ways of inhabiting a land that we all claim to love.

On the way back from our summer visit to the Beitillu Nature Reserve near Ramallah, we drive by the Um Safa forest where we once strolled and picnicked. An iron gate now forbids entry; the forest is now the preserve of an Israeli settlement and renamed Neve Tsuf. But the forest remains, waiting, I think, for the gate to be opened.

SOURCES AND RESOURCES

INTRODUCTION: COMMON LIVES

Cavell, Stanley. "Companionable Thinking." In *Philosophy and Animal Life*, edited by Cary Wolfe. New York: Columbia University Press, 2008.

De Waal, Frans. *Are We Smart Enough to Know How Smart Animals Are?* New York: W.W. Norton and Company, 2016.

Diamond, Cora. "Eating Meat and Eating People." *Philosophy* 53, no. 206 (October 1978): 465–479.

Mankell, Henning. *Quicksand: What It Means to Be a Human Being*. London: Vintage, 2017.

Mikhail, Alan, ed. *Water on Sand: Environmental Histories of the Middle East*. Oxford: Oxford University Press, 2013.

Morell, Virginia. *Animal Wise: How We Know Animals Think and Feel*. New York: Broadway Books, 2013.

Qumsiyeh, Mazin B. *Mammals of the Holy Land*. Lubbock, TX: Texas Tech University Press, 1996.

Thomas, Chris D. *Inheritors of the Earth: How Nature Is Thriving in an Age of Extinction*. New York: Public Affairs, 2017.

Zeuner, Frederick E. *A History of the Domestication of Animals*. New York: Harper and Row, 1963.

CHAPTER 1: TAKE MY CAMEL:
THE VANISHING CAMELS OF JERUSALEM AND JAFFA

Al-Ahari, Mohammed. "The Story of Hajj Ali and the U.S. Camel Calvary Corps." *Chicago Monitor*, March 8, 2016.

Barr, James. *A Line in the Sand: Britain, France and the Struggle that Shaped the Middle East.* London: Simon and Schuster, 2011.

Ben-Bassat, Yuval. *Petitioning the Sultan: Protests and Justice in Late Ottoman Palestine.* London: I.B. Tauris, 2013.

Berda, Yael. *Living Emergency: Israel's Permit Regime in the Occupied West Bank.* Redwood City, 07: Stanford University Press, 2018.

Boullata, Kamal. *Between Exits: Paintings by Hani Zurob.* London: Black Dog, 2012.

Bulliet, Richard W. *The Camel and the Wheel.* Cambridge: Cambridge University Press, 1975.

Casto, E. Ray. "Economic Geography of Palestine." *Economic Geography* 23 (1937): 235–259.

Davidson, Robyn. *Tracks: A Woman's Solo Trek Across 1,700 Miles of Australian Outback.* New York: Vintage Departures Editions, 2014.

Davis, Rochelle. "The Growth of the Western Communities, 1917–1948." In *Jerusalem 1948: The Arab Neighborhoods and Their Fate in the War,* edited by Salim Tamari. Jerusalem: Institute of Jerusalem Studies, and Bethlehem: Badil Resource Center for Palestinian Residency and Refugee Rights, 1999.

El-Eini, Roza. *Mandated Landscape: British Imperial Rule in Palestine, 1929–1948.* London and New York: Routledge, 2006.

Falah, Ghazi. *The Role of the British Administration in the Sedentarization of Bedouin Tribes in Northern Palestine.* Durham: University of Durham, Center for Middle East and Islamic Studies, 1983.

Flaubert, Gustave. *Flaubert in Egypt.* London: Penguin, 1996.

Gitler, Inbal. "'Marrying Modern Progress with Treasured Antiquity': Jerusalem City Plans During the British Mandate, 1917–1948." *Traditional Dwellings and Settlements Review* 15 (2003): 39–58.

Hadawi, Sami. "Sodomy, Locusts, and Cholera: A Jerusalem Witness." *Jerusalem Quarterly* 52 (Spring 2013): 7–27.

Hawkins, Vince. "The U.S. Army's 'Camel Corps' Experiment." National Museum of the U.S. Army Campaign online, July 16, 2014. https://armyhistory.org/the-u-s-armys-camel-corps -experiment.

Howells, Victor. *A Naturalist in Palestine*. New York: Philosophical Library, 1956.

Inchbald, Geoffrey. *Imperial Camel Corps*. London: Johnson, 1970.

Irwin, Robert. *Camel*. London: Reaktion Books, 2010.

Khalidi, Walid. *Before Their Diaspora: A Photographic History of the Palestinians 1876–1948*. Washington, Institute of Palestine Studies, 1984.

Khalili, Laleh. "The Location of Palestine in Global Counterinsurgencies." *International Journal of Middle Eastern Studies* 42 (2010): 413–433.

Macaulay, Rose. *The Towers of Trebizond*. New York: New York Review Books, 2003.

Montefiore, Simon Sebag. *Jerusalem: The Biography*. London: Weidenfeld and Nicolson, 2011.

Pullan, Wendy, and Lefkos Kyriacou. "The Work of Charles Ashbee: Ideological Urban Visions with Everyday City Spaces." *Jerusalem Quarterly* 39 (2009).

CHAPTER 2: MAMMALS BEHAVING BADLY: HYENAS, HUMANS, AND TALES OF FEAR AND LOATHING

Rogers, Mary Eliza. *Domestic Life in Palestine*. London: Kegan Paul International, 1989, first published London: Bell and Daldy, 1862.

Thompson, Ken. *Where Do Camels Belong?: The Story and Science of Invasive Species*. London: Profile Books, 2014.

Abdel Fattah, et al. "Wild Mammals in the Gaza Strip, with Particular Reference to Wadi Gaza." *The Islamic University Journal* (Series of Natural Studies and Engineering) 25, no. 1 (2007): 87–109.

Albaba, Imadeddin Moh'd. "A Primary Survey of the Striped Hyaena, *Hyaena hyaena*, (Linnaeus, 1758), (Carnivora: Hyaenidae) Status in the West Bank Governorates, Palestine." Global Scholastic Research Journal 1, no. 10 (September 2015): 39–44.

Baynes-Rock, Marcus. *Among the Bone Eaters: Encounters with Hyenas in Harar*. Philadelphia: University of Pennsylvania Press, 2015.

Berger, John. "Why Look at Animals?" In his *About Looking*. London: Bloomsbury, 2009.

Brulliaird, Karin. "Wolves and Hyenas Hunt Together, Prove Middle East Peace Is Possible." *Washington Post*, March 10, 2016.

Darwish, Najwan. "Reserved." In *Nothing More to Lose*, translated by Kareem James Abu Zeid. New York: New York Review Books, 2014.

Dinets, Vladimir, and Benjamin Eligulashvili. "Striped Hyenas (*Hyaena hyaena*) in Grey Wolf (*Canis lupus*) Packs: Cooperation, Communalism or Singular Aberration?" *Zoology in the Middle East* 62, no. 1 (2016): 85–87.

Dubosc, Dominique. "Dream of the Hyena," a film, Hebron 2007. Posted on Palestine Calling: vimeo.com/40538280.

Johnson, Penny. "Tales of Strength and Danger: Sahar and the Tactics of Everyday Life in Amari Refugee Camp, Palestine." *Signs: Journal of Women in Culture and Society* 32, no. 3 (2007).

Palestine Environmental Authority. "National Biodiversity Strategy and Action Plan for Palestine." Hebron, January 1999.

Sayigh, Rosemary, ed. *Yusuf Sayigh: Arab Economist and Palestinian Patriot*. Cairo and New York: The American University in Cairo Press, 2015.

Thomas, Amelia. *The Zoo on the Road to Nablus: A Story of Survival from the West Bank*. New York: Public Affairs, 2007.

Tristram, H. B. *Survey of Western Palestine (1882–1888): The Fauna and Flora of Palestine.* Cambridge: Cambridge Archive Editions, 1998. Originally published London: Committee of the Palestine Exploration Fund, 1884.

CHAPTER 3: FLOCKS BY DAY: GOATS, SHEEP, AND SHEPHERDS UNDER THREAT

Cole, Teju. "Bad Laws." In his *Known and Strange Things.* London: Faber and Faber, 2016.

El-Eini, Roza. "The Implementation of British Agricultural Policy in Palestine in the 1930s."*Middle Eastern Studies* 32 (1996): 211–250.

———. "British Forestry Policy in Mandatory Palestine, 1929–1948: Aims and Realities," *Middle Eastern Studies* 35 (1999): 72–149.

Goor, A. Y. "Ten Years After." *Empire Forestry Review* 37, no. 4 (December 1958): 418–420.

Hareuveni, Eyal. "Dispossession and Exploitation: Israel's Policy in the Jordan Valley and Northern Dead Sea. Jerusalem: B'tselem, May 2011.

Hinson, Joy. *Goat.* London: Reaktion Books, 2015.

Hlelhel, Ala. "Bloated Time and the Death of Meaning." In *Kingdom of Olives and Ashes: Writers Confront the Occupation*, edited by Michael Chabon and Ayelet Waldman. New York: Harper Perennial, 2017.

Shami, Yitzhaq. *Hebron Stories.* Lancaster, CA: Labyrinthos, 2000.

Thwaites, Thomas. *GoatMan: How I Took a Holiday from Being Human.* New York: Princeton Architectural Press, 2016.

CHAPTER 4: I WISH I WAS A DONKEY . . . OR DO I?

Berger, John. "Why Look at Animals?" In his *About Looking.* London: Bloomsbury, 2009.

Bough, Jill. *Donkey.* London: Reaktion Books, 2011.

Merrifield, Andy. *The Wisdom of Donkeys: Finding Tranquility in a Chaotic World*. New York: Walker and Company, 2008.

Sardur, Ziauddin. *Mecca: The Sacred City*. London: Bloomsbury, 2014.

Stevenson, Robert Louis. *Travels with a Donkey in the Cevennes*. London: Penguin Classics, 2004.

Twain, Mark. *Innocents Abroad*. Knoxville: Wordsworth Classics, 2010.

CHAPTER 5: WHERE ARE WE GOING, RIVKA?: COWS IN AN OCCUPIED ECONOMY

Bishop, Elizabeth. "Santarém." In *The Complete Poems 1927–1979*. London: Hogarth Press, 1984.

Hardy, Thomas. *Tess of the d'Urbervilles*. London: Macmillian, 1970.

Netanyahu, Benjamin. "Address by PM Netanyahu at the 2015 Genesis Prize Ceremony." Prime Minister's Office online. http://www.pmo.gov.il/English/MediaCenter/Speeches/Pages /speechBereshit180615.aspx.

Shomali, Amer, and Paul Cowan. *The Wanted 18*. National Film Board of Canada and Kino Lerber, 2014. Canada/France/Palestine.

Tal, Alon. "Enduring Technological Optimism: Zionism's Environmental Ethic and Its Influence on Israel's Environmental History." *Environmental History* 13 (April 2008): 275–305.

———. *Pollution in a Promised Land: An Environmental History of Israel*. Berkeley: University of California Press, 2002.

World Bank Group. "Palestine's Economic Prospects." Washington: World Bank, Spring 2016.

———. "Prospects for Growth of Jobs in The Palestinian Economy." Washington, World Bank, 2018.

CHAPTER 6: A CONSPIRACY OF WILD BOARS

Abulafia, David. *The Great Sea: A Human History of the Mediterranean*. London: Penguin Books, 2013.

Albaba, Imadeddin Moh'd. "The Impact of Wild Boar (*Sus scrofa*) on Different Agricultural Crops in the Northern Governorates of Palestine." *International Journal of Fauna and Biological Studies* (October 2016): 25–27.

Auden, W. H. "In Praise of Limestone." In *Selected Poems*. Edited by Edward Mendelson. London: Faber and Faber, 1979.

Cohen, Shaul. "Environmentalism Deferred: Nationalism and Israeli /Palestinian Imaginaries." In *Environmental Imaginaries of the Middle East and North Africa*. Edited by Diana K. David and Edmund Burke III. Athens, OH: Ohio University Press, 2011.

Homer. *The Odyssey*. Translated by Martin Hammond. London: Gerald Duckworth and Co., 2000.

Wohlleben, Peter. *The Inner Life of Animals: Surprising Observations of a Hidden World*. London: Bodley Head, 2017.

CHAPTER 7: THE HOWL OF THE JACKAL

Adorno, Theodor. "Notes on Kafka." In his *Prisms*. Cambridge, MA: MIT Press, 1983.

Flores, Dan. *Coyote America: A Natural and Supernatural History*. New York: Basic Books, 2016.

Green, David. "Big Trouble in Little Palestine: Britain's Rough Three Decades in the Holy Land." *Ha'aretz* newspaper, June 23, 2018.

Hanssen, Jens. "Kafka and Arabs." *Critical Inquiry* 39, Autumn 2012: 167–197

Kafka, Franz. "Jackals and Arabs," *Franz Kafka: The Complete Stories*. New York: Schocken Books, 1971.

Oz, Amos. *A Tale of Love and Darkness*. New York: Harcourt 2005.

———. *Where the Jackals Howl*. London: Flamingo, 1980.

Wood, Ramsay. *Kalila and Dimna: Fables of Friendship and Betrayal*. Introduction by Doris Lessing. London: Saqi, 2008.

CHAPTER 8: STILL WILD: GAZELLES, IBEXES, AND WOLVES

Darwish, Mahmoud. "If I Were a Hunter." Translated by Shakir Mustafa. ArabLit (blog), March 13, 2016. https://arab lit.org/2016/03/13/on-mahmoud-darwishs-birthday-a-new -translation-of-if-i-were-a-hunter.

Flannery, Tim. "Raised by Wolves." *New York Review of Books* 65, no. 6 (April 5–, 2018).

Kreiger, Barbara. *The Dead Sea and the Jordan River.* Bloomington: Indiana University Press, 2016.

Lopez, Barry. *Of Wolves and Men.* New York: Scribner, 2004.

Mikhail, Alan. *The Animal in Ottoman Egypt.* Oxford: Oxford University Press, 2014

O'Brien, Vanessa. "Israeli Army Opens West Bank Barrier for Animals." Deutsche Welle, November 2, 2012. https://www .dw.com/en/israeli-army-opens-west-bank-barrier-for-animals /a-16351700.

Price, Max D., Austin C. Hill, Yorke M. Rowan, and Morag M. Kersel. "Gazelles, Liminality, and Chalcolithic Ritual: A Case Study from Marj Rabba, Israel." *Bulletin of the American School of Oriental Research* no. 376 (November 2016): 7–27.

Stuart, Chris, and Tilde Stuart. *Mammals of North Africa and the Middle East.* London: Bloomsbury, 2016.

Yom-Tov, Yoram. "Human Impact on Wildlife in Israel Since the Nineteenth Century" In *Between Ruin and Restoration: An Environmental History of Israel.* Edited by Daniel Orenstein, Alon Tal, and Char Miller. Pittsburgh: University of Pittsburgh Press, 2013.

CONCLUSION: THE WORST ZOO IN THE WORLD: LIVES IN COMMON?

Amr, Zuhair, et al. "Change in Diet of the Eurasian Eagle Owl (*Bubo bubo*) Suggest Decline in Biodiversity in Wadi Al Makhrour,

Bethlehem Governorate, Palestinian Territories." *Slovak Raptor Journal* 10, no. 1 (2016): 75–79.

Eagleton, Terry. *Hope Without Optimism*. New Haven: Yale University Press, 2016.

Hass, Amira. "What Luck It Is to Be a Tiger in Gaza," *Ha'aretz* newspaper, October 3, 2016.

Lear, Jonathan. *Radical Hope: Ethics in the Face of Cultural Devastation.* Cambridge, MA: Harvard University Press, 2006.

Purdy, Jedediah. *After Nature: A Politics for the Anthropocene.* Cambridge, MA: Harvard University Press, 2015.

Qumsiyeh, Mazin, and Ziad Amr. *Environmental Conservation and Protected Areas in Palestine: Challenges and Opportunities.* Bethlehem: Hans Seidel Foundation, 2018.

Safi, Ahmed. "On the 'IDF's Vegan Warriors': A Vegan Palestinian's Perspective." Palestinian Animal League online, February 5, 2016. https://pal.ps/en/2016/02/05/on-the-idfs-vegan-warriors-a-vegan-palestinians-perspective/.

Thomas, Chris D. *Inheritors of the Earth: How Nature is Thriving in an Age of Extinction.* New York: Public Affairs, 2017.

RESOURCES: WILDLIFE, ANIMAL WELFARE, AND ENVIRONMENTAL ORGANIZATIONS IN PALESTINE

Environmental Education Center: eecp.org

Palestinian Animal League: pal.ps

Palestine Institute for Biodiversity and Sustainability and Palestinian Museum of Natural History: palestinenature.org

Palestine Wildlife Society: wildlife-pal.org

ACKNOWLEDGMENTS

Thanks to all my walking and exploring partners, particularly: Bassam, Salma, and Adam Almohor; Susan Rockwell; Rema Hammami; Alex Pollack; George Al'Ama; Carol Khoury; Salwa Daibis; and Gerard Horton. Salwa and Gerard, another thank-you both for getting me into the military court at Ofer and for your exemplary work at Military Court Watch. My great appreciation for the assistance of Rana Hanoun in allowing me to accompany field visits of the Food and Agriculture Organization, and to Amro Kalouti and Intissar Eshtayah as companions and guides on these highly informative occasions. Thanks and admiration to those who gave me photographs and images: Bassam Almohor, Emile Ashrawi, Imad Atrash, Gerard Horton, and Amer Shomali, whose animated cows continue to delight me. My many earlier walks with the Shat-ha walking group, ably led by Samia al Botmeh and Saleh Abdul Jawad, offered numerous encounters with the animals, people and landscapes of Palestine which have informed this book. The invaluable assistance and persistence of Dr. Sami Khader, chief veterinarian of the Qalqilya zoo, and Saleh Afaneh, engineer at the Salfit municipality, evoke both my gratitude and admiration. For introducing me to the amazing work of Palestinian environmental and animal welfare and wildlife activists and experts, I warmly thank Simon Awad of the Environmental Education Center, Dr. Mazin Qumsiyeh and the dedicated volunteers at the Institute for Biodiversity and Sustainability/ Museum of Natural History, Ahmed Safi and his colleagues at the Palestinian Animal League, and Imad Atrash and Ibrahim Odeh of the Palestine Wildlife Society. Dr. Adala Attireh and Dr. Issa at the Environmental Quality Agency and Dr. Iyad Adra at the Ministry of Agriculture offered me a window into the difficulties of protecting environment and animals in Palestine under the limited mandate and resources of the Palestine Authority, as well as furthering my appreciation of their hard work to do the same. My agent George Lucas's encouragement and sage advice was vital to commencing this book, and Ryan Harrington, my astute editor at Melville House Books, in completing it.

And as always, Raja Shehadeh.

INDEX